MIRACULOUS

MIRACULOUS

My journey from hell to heaven.

Lena Cebula

XULON PRESS

Xulon Press
2301 Lucien Way #415
Maitland, FL 32751
407.339.4217
www.xulonpress.com

Printed in the United States of America.

ISBN-13: 9781545673409

Table of Contents

Acknowledgements

I am so grateful to God that He gave me an opportunity to tell my story. I hope and pray you will see that Jesus loves you and He doesn't make exceptions. I have so much gratitude for my amazing husband. Thank you for loving me unconditionally all these years. Thank you to my beautiful children, you are my precious gifts from God. You made me a mother, a title that I wear so proudly. Thank you Tom, for taking care of me better than my parents ever did. Thank you to my mother-in-law, for your love, wisdom, joy, and guidance and to the rest of my family for loving me and praying for me. Many thanks to my church family and friends, your support and prayers are amazing. And a special thank you to my beautiful sister-in-law, who helped shape and polish this story of mine. Love to all of you who read this book - I am so grateful for you! May God Almighty bless you and your beautiful families with peace, love and joy.

Chapter 1

Beauty for Ashes

Therefore, if anyone is in Christ, he is a new creation; the old has gone, the new has come!
2 Corinthians 15:17, NIV

The Spirit of the Sovereign LORD is on me, because the LORD has anointed me to proclaim good news to the poor... to bestow on them a crown of beauty instead of ashes, the oil of joy instead of mourning, and a garment of praise instead of a spirit of despair.
Isaiah 61:1-3, NIV

*L*ooking back on my life, reflecting on where I've come from, where I am now, and where I am going, I can tell you that these verses are absolutely true! *Beauty for ashes* that's what I've got; such change I would never think possible in my lifetime. Sometimes, I can't even believe the life I've lived, almost as if when I'm remembering pieces, I'm watching them happen to someone else. Some of my memories play more like a horror movie than simple

1

recollections. Regardless of what I've been through, what flashes of horror invade my life now, I know that I am truly healed, *a new creation.*

I was neglected as a child and grew into a lost and angry teenager looking for meaning and belonging wherever I thought it could be found. By the time I was in my mid-twenties, I was hopeless, alone, empty, broken, and living in constant fear. One day everything changed. I gave my life to Christ and chose to follow Him. It was a long, hard road to walk but somewhere along the way I became a loving wife and mother to three beautiful children. I knew I was cherished and embraced by a God who gave his life for me and a husband who would do anything for me. I was whole and lived in the security of the hope that is Christ. God's timing is perfect and his grace amazing. I would not be who I am today without the turbulent experiences of the early years of my life. For that, I am genuinely grateful for everything I experienced. My mother always used to say that life wasn't whatever *happened* to you, it was what you *made* out of whatever happened to you. This was her atheistic mantra, positive thinking, use everything as an opportunity to learn etc... Not for all the positive thinking in the world could I have turned my past into something beautiful, only the grace of God could do that.

If I had only known growing up that I had a perfect Father, I would have avoided doing half of the stuff I did in my life. Occasionally I share bits and pieces of my life with friends, the lessons I've learned. I enjoy talking about times when God has been faithful to me. But these were usually things in my recent past, things that happened to me since becoming a Christian and they were usually shared with people I knew and trusted. I never thought God would ask me to share my story – my *whole* story – with the world. In fact, if I didn't feel that God had directly asked me to write this book I would probably bury my history, never giving it a chance to see the light of day. I had a carefully crafted story that was honest enough, it covered the basics without anything incriminating. I grew up in Ukraine, moved to Israel, then immigrated to Canada – simple! Within this, people understood that my upbringing was rough, but I often lied to avoid questions about just how rough it really was, scared of rejection and judgment. But God has a plan for me and for my broken past as well. Even if it looked like a mess in the beginning it has a beautiful ending... well, not quite yet. I'm still currently enjoying the middle!

I can remember the day I finally decided to be vulnerable and share everything. It was a Sunday. My oldest daughter took her younger twin siblings downstairs and made them breakfast. For the first time in a long time I was laying fully awake in my bed with no one screaming "mommy!". It was a wonderful feeling. I stretched lazily in my warm comfy bed, listening to the rain fall outside. Moments of quiet reflection like this seemed to happen rarely. My thoughts drifted to my past – the memories and all the feelings that are attached to those memories flooded me. I never just remember facts, I absorb the feeling of a moment and relive it later on, probably why I hate horror movies! I get stuck in the fear, reliving the panic long after it's been copied into my brain. This propensity to get immersed in old feelings is partly why I always blocked out my past, even from myself to an extent. You see, these vivid memories are a double-edged sword; sometimes it's great, like remembering the smell of a forest or a field on a hot summers day when you're actually stuck shoveling your driveway after *another* snow storm. Other times it's awful – you're transported to a place you never asked to be!

On this particular morning I was not experiencing a pleasant memory – a strange contrast to my very peaceful morning. Instead of being in my warm, comfy bed I was back in Ukraine, where I grew up. I was very young and had lost the keys to our apartment. My father was very angry, lost his temper, and began beating me with a belt. I bounced from painful memory to painful memory, wondering why this cycle of misery was playing out in my mind and body.

I started to feel uneasy. All I wanted was a nice peaceful morning while I got ready for church. I complained to my husband that I had felt tricked by God. I was sure that he wanted me to share my story and his miracles in my life, but I wasn't ready to discuss all the pain that lead to those miracles. I was already half-way through my first draft of this very book, and yet there was not a single detail from my past in any of the pages. I didn't agree to put my misery on display, I was writing this book to highlight all the good that had happened to me!

That's when I felt a nudge, "You weren't born a Christian, 35-year-old mother of 3 kids with a wonderful husband and house in the suburbs. This is only a *part* of your story. There is a long beginning you have to wrestle with... ". I broke down crying. I really didn't feel prepared. I assumed my book would be all sunshine and rainbows, making people feel warm and fuzzy. Unfortunately, my life has been far from sunshine and rainbows.

I turned to my husband, with tears in my eyes, and asked him how much he knew about my past. He answered truthfully that he did not know *all* of my story. Not that I hadn't tried to tell him; before our wedding I wrote him a letter detailing all that I had been through, all that I had done. I wanted to be honest with him. I wanted him to know exactly who he was marrying so that he never felt hoodwinked. Perhaps some part of me still didn't believe I deserved such happiness, so I was giving him one last chance to escape. I gave him the letter I wrote, but he refused to read it. "Whatever is in this letter is between you and God. I love you for who you are now. Pray about this letter, then burn it". Exhaling with relief, I took the letter back and destroyed it thinking we'd never have to discuss my past again, but my time has come.

Chapter 2

Olenushka

I was born in a modern culturally Russian city right in the middle of Ukraine. Geologists discovered rich deposits of iron in the land that surrounded my city so many families, like my own, immigrated from Russia to work in the mines and factories that were created to process this newly discovered resource. That's how my city was born. It was young, with no glamorous history like it's surrounding neighbours, but it was *my* city. It will always have a special place in my heart. But it was a complex time to live in Ukraine. I experienced all the common hardships my city had to offer – cramped living conditions, smog from the factories, little access to heated water – but I was also gifted with its beauty; wide open fields, massive skies, streams and brooks to play in. In many ways it was a child's paradise.

Little Olenushka, my grandparents lovingly called me. Nothing about me was little though - I was born an explorer, with dreams to see the world! I always carried a sense of wonder with me wherever I went. Leaving my house early in the morning, I would wander to the beach, explore the forests, sneak into the factories, and hide out in the mines. My friends and I would scurry along the train tracks, climb over piles of rubble, and stare in awe at the heavy machinery all around us. While I loved nature, it was also fascinating to see what humans were capable of as well. The mines and factories felt as large as entire cities and often there was a black cloud of soot enveloping the area, especially after mine explosions. The earth and houses shook, but it was the norm. Soot, loud machinery and dirt were all very familiar to me.

My mother worked in a factory operating a crane and assembled other equipment. She was a pro at what she did. One time, the city discovered that there was sunken World War II tank at the bottom of the river that ran through my city. My mother was in charge of bringing it to the surface and restoring it so that it could be used in a monument. She let me climb inside the corroded body to explore – nothing but rust and empty bullet shells, but I loved it. I had strong imagination and playing around inside this tank made me proud of my country.

Looking back, there probably should have been some boundaries for safety and maybe there was, but they were never imposed on me. The factories were my playground, but also my home in a sense. For many people, the factory where you worked became your life. It was where you bathed (one of the few places that provided hot water!), where you socialized (they had pool tables and a swimming pool), and even where you got some rest (they had a sauna). Everyone worked very long hours, so the factory met these other basic needs as a courtesy. I would come before my mother's shift would end and collect fabric scraps and I would use these scraps to make outfits for my dolls. It was exciting to score big pieces with print or anything shiny I could use as an accessory. I designed the outfits and sowed everything myself. My sowing skills weren't just for the luxury of my dolls, it was a necessary skill for myself – I had to mend my own clothes!

My friends were the best part of my childhood. We relished in having this absolute freedom to go where we pleased. I recognize it now as neglect – we were orphans with parents – but at the time it was intoxicating. In summer we were dirty and covered in sweat, in winter we were soaking wet and frozen to the core. No one owned snow pants or proper gloves, of course. We would scavenge for pieces of cardboard or plastic bags that we could use to toboggan down ice covered hills, hills I would never let my kids go down now! High, steep, rocky and very close to the road. There was no hot chocolate and a movie waiting for me when I got home, nor did our parents ever ask what we were up to. We were completely alone. One year, the city council decided to build a church. I could not care less that it was a church they were building, but the construction zone became our favourite playground. We'd wander through the half-built building, jumping from beams, playing hide and seek in the labyrinthine basement.

We were hungry – always hungry- but we were also happy. To have a crew to do life with was amazing. Our homes weren't that great, so we made our own imaginary one out of the old, gigantic willow tree that grew in front of our building. There was no fear, no stress, no bullying, and no loneliness – we were there for each other. These were the sunny days before my country's economy collapsed and my parents' marriage fell apart... I would never again look back on my childhood with fondness after that.

Chapter 3

My Parents

I often think a lot about my parents, my father especially. What I know of him is only fragments, pieced together by memories and things I've learned after his death. He was a quiet and simple man who loved being in nature. He left his dream life behind and settled into a mundane city life and boring factory job to be with my mom. He never told us that he was one of the first USSR mountain climbers who climbed Everest. (I read the article from a newspaper saved in his album a few years after he died).

My mother, on the other hand, hated nature; she was 100% a city girl, the complete opposite of my dad. She was stubborn and dominating, a trademark of being the first born of her family and a trait that seems to trickle down the generations. My mother suffered from my grandma's desire to dominate and control and couldn't wait to escape her controlling grip. Once my mom was free from the control of my grandmother, no one could tell her what to do and as a result, I suffered. Now that I have my own daughters, they also suffer – at times I can be controlling and demanding of obedience. I learned from their mistakes while creating scores of my own until I recognized this pattern of control snaking it's way through my family history like a river with no end.

Despite these differences, my dad gave up everything for my mom... and me. My mother got pregnant with me before she married my dad and while she was still living at home. Her parents didn't approve of their relationship and tried to convince her to stay, but, always looking for an escape, my mom married my dad as way out. Once married, she considered the responsibilities of a wife and mother to be a burden. Because it felt like a burden, she figured she had made a mistake in marrying my father, so divorced him when my sister and I were very little. Once divorced, she realized raising kids and keeping a home without my dad was even more of a burden. She got back together with my dad, but it didn't last. It was a relationship of convenience for her, not love. She was unwilling to change, compromise, and communicate -all things necessary for a marriage to work. She partied with friends and left my father at home to take care of the cleaning & cooking. His male pride and dignity completely trampled over day by day. His friends and community often poked fun at the fact that he was the only man in town with a stroller. It didn't matter to me that my father was the housekeeper, my mother was a terrible cook and even worse cleaner, but I came to resent my father's weakness. I couldn't understand how he stood by while my mother acted the way she did.

Not that my father was perfect. Whenever my dad would confront my mom regarding her behavior, insults would fly, and tensions would rise. Many fights turned physical. Back home it wasn't uncommon for a husband to hit his wife, but for my dad it was unacceptable behavior. He was upset that he lost control. My mother had a big black eye. I saw this and vowed never to marry a man who would beat me. Such violence back then was so common that if my mother had told people what really happened, it wouldn't be a big deal. But she was a proud woman, telling everyone that a suitcase had fallen on her face instead.

I was never certain how my father would react to things and this uncertainty made me live on edge. I could do one thing one day with no consequences and do the same thing the next day with disastrous consequences. Abuse – verbal and physical – was my reality. One time, I broke a crystal vase and was so afraid that I locked myself in the bath-room. There, I prayed to God, who I only knew about from Christmas songs. I said: "God if you truly exist, please don't let my dad beat me again!" I wasn't sure if it was enough, so I stuffed a small pillow into my pants to protect my butt. When my dad came home, I bravely confessed to my crime, emboldened by the protective pillow I had in my pants. To my surprise, my dad did nothing. I considered this a mir-acle and attributed it to my bathroom cry for help. I had a sense that God had heard me. If only I knew then God really was with me…

Shortly after this incident, my father quit his job. I wish I could say I knew why, but I don't. He then started drinking heavily and became an alcoholic. While my father seemed to be crumbling, my mother didn't care. My father was pulling the weight of both parents until he finally snapped. That's when the drinking began.

Because of my parent's negligence, we fell into debt and lost everything we had. The government cut off our electricity and hot water. With my parents out of work we owed money for rent and had no food for days. Our house was infested with mold and cockroaches. When my kids say that we have "no food" or that they have "nothing to wear", I get angry. They don't know that nothing to eat means an empty fridge for months. Starving means your stomach is so empty that the pain makes you dizzy. "Nothing to wear "means your only outfit, already dirty and threadbare, doesn't even keep you warm. My parents were exceptional actors though, pretending to all our friends and family that everything was fine.

Desperate for a paycheck and a hopeless drunk, my dad went to Moscow for a construction job. I was almost 14 , my sister 12, and my brother 7. With my dad gone, my mother suddenly disappeared without a trace. It hit me that they abandoned us in an empty, cold, dark apartment with no means to survive. Eventually I would quit school. I was embarrassed of my old, dirty, stinky clothes and always-hungry stomach. On top of all I had to take care of my siblings. For a while I was their mother. I couldn't find the words to explain to my baby brother that our parents were both gone and that I didn't know where they were and when they would be back. That's when my childhood was stolen.

I've spent so much of my life judging my parents for the decisions they made, but I've come to see how the choices were made in a place of desperation and brokenness. I expected love and protection when they had none for themselves. My anger gave way to pity when I finally realized this.

Chapter 4

My Grandparents

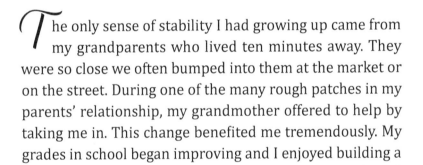

The only sense of stability I had growing up came from my grandparents who lived ten minutes away. They were so close we often bumped into them at the market or on the street. During one of the many rough patches in my parents' relationship, my grandmother offered to help by taking me in. This change benefited me tremendously. My grades in school began improving and I enjoyed building a relationship with my grandma. I loved the bond I had forged with my grandma, but my mother hated it and became very jealous.

My grandmother's house was different – there were rules and discipline. I resisted this strict new home at first, but my grandmother also compromised. With age comes wisdom, so by the time my grandmother took me in she had seen the consequences of raising her own daughter with too much control – she had pushed her own daughter away. With me, she learned, adopted and adjusted giving me the best of herself. She was softer on me than she had ever been on my mom – this caused a lot of tension between my mom and I – but, she was still strict. School work was always a priority. If I refused to do it, she would threaten to lock me in the dark bathroom with mice. It worked every time, whether she was serious or not.

They had a beautiful apricot tree that would bloom in their yard. When ripe, my grandpa would shake the stump and big orange apricots would fall to the ground. Neighborhood kids would run and pick them up, putting them into their pockets with giggles and delight. We would eat them dirty, straight from the ground. No one ever told us to wash our fruits or hands. So, it was a strict upbringing but also had carefree moments.

My grandparents married young. They were a beautiful couple. My grandpa had this defiant fire in him that could make him difficult to get along with, but my grandma loved him. She forgave all his mistakes and stood by him no matter what. The nature of his work was always unclear to me. I knew that people in my city respected and feared him. His tattoos and the fact that he served jailed time told me that he was 'someone'. Apart from that, I knew nothing. I feared him when I was little, but once I witnessed my grandpa head-butt a guy so hard, blood came pouring from the other guy's face. Rather than get scared, I swelled with pride and took this display of violence as proof of my grandpa's authority. It comforted me to know he was respected. Violence and dominance were my barometers for success.

My grandpa quickly became the central male figure in my life. He taught me important life lessons about choices and consequences and gave me the freedom to speak my mind. He and my grandma loved me. No one else in my family had this kind of relationship with my grandparents.

I saw my grandpa as strong and gentle and my grandma as strict and wise. I saw the way they treated each other, the way they made decisions and dealt with problems. It wasn't always great, and it took them 20 years of marriage to figure out how to live and thrive as a couple. I asked her once how she could live that long with the same guy. She smiled, "One day you will fall in love and years will fly..."

They were completely committed to each other. Their reward? 52 years together, 2 children, 5 grandchildren, 11 great children and 1 great great child - a huge family tree! They were the only ones in my family with a successful marriage. Looking up to them, I decided I could never settle for anything less than what they had. But, even though we were close, my life went in a direction I had to hide from them. It broke my heart to lie to them, but I knew it would break *their* hearts to know the truth.

Chapter 5

School

*G*oing to school for me was tumultuous. I loved to read and learn new things, but all I wanted was for my mother to be proud. I wanted her to recognize me, affirm me, and give me the attention I so craved. I also wanted to become a police officer - I was fascinated with the uniform and authority it imposed - and was told that you needed high grades for that. So, I worked hard for straight A's, convinced that those A's would make my mother proud and bring me closer to my goal of being a police officer.

While my grades did nothing to impress my mother, I became disenchanted. Striving no longer seemed worth the effort. I had also made some dangerous friends. We would bully other kids and cause trouble just because. One time, I got drunk and was picked up by the cops and taken to jail – my first encounter. Rather than give me a warning, they beat me. My faith broken in the police system, I decided I didn't want to be a police officer anymore. I wanted to be beyond the law, untouchable.

As my school life was deteriorating, so was my home life...or was it the other way around? It's hard to know for sure. My parents – oblivious to my hard work at school – would throw wild parties late into the night. The cacophony of smoking, screaming, swearing, and drunken cackles became my lullaby as I tried to sleep. I became a product of my environment and myself started smoking at age 13, swearing so much I could put sailors to shame. The school staff became concerned and brought my mother in to talk about me. When they told my mother that I had started smoking and was generally uncontrollable, my mother sarcastically replied, "I guess I should start giving her money so she can actually afford the cigarettes". The shock on the teachers' faces was unforgettable. Now, I pity my younger self but at the time a pride swelled within me, I really *was* uncontrollable, accountable to no one! I hid nothing from my parents – what was there to hide? I was only doing what they were doing.

I had no rules and no curfew. This parenting style appealed to my friends. They liked that I never got in trouble and they especially liked that they never got in trouble when they were with me. While they admired my life, I was envious that they had someone who cared about them, someone to be worried for them when they didn't come home, someone to call them home for dinner and make sure they got a good night's sleep before school the next day. I would stay at my friends' house for days at a time – my parents never even wondered where I was.

Because no one took care of me, I didn't know my worth, especially when it came to the worth of my own body. Thanks to what my mother called our 'modern upbringing' I was never told that sex could be something special. Modesty

– what was that? A concept I had never known. I was only 14 when I had sex for the first time. I really only did it because my friend was doing it. I found the act weird and a little gross. When my friend's mom found out she was no longer a virgin, she freaked out. My mom? She said nothing ... then started dating the guy a little while later.

All this neglect was starting to show. I was dirty and had no clothes to wear. Hungry and embarrassed I began missing school a lot. Monthly nurses would check our class for lice. Being pulled out from class in front of everybody was humiliating because everyone knew that meant they found lice. You can imagine how many times I was pulled out. My mother often shaved my head to deal with this problem. When I got older she poured gasoline on my head to kill lice so I could keep my hair. I stunk for days and everyone knew why. My tights were mended so many times at the bottom that it hurt my toes. My clothes and shoes were either a size too small or too big; nothing fit properly. The height of my humility was hitting puberty though. I had no one to talk me through the changes my body was experiencing and no bra to hide those changes. Kids started making fun of me, so I quickly developed a tough skin and aggressive personality to protect myself.

I was starving most of the time and was lucky to have anything to eat at all. I learned to hustle to get food for myself and to feed my brother and sister. I had to lie and steal just in order to survive. My teacher suspected as much and after I failed a few exams she came to my house to check in on me. She told my mother that I had great potential but that I just needed parental control and guidance. My mother never cared what I needed and couldn't stand having someone tell her what to do that she sent my teacher away without hope of anything changing.

Not only was the neglect showing, it was starting to poison me on the inside. I became angry and violent. I resented other kids my age who were more fortunate than I and would find myself punishing them just for existing. I got into lots of fights, starting many of them. Most of the time there was no consequence to my violence, but sometimes I chose the wrong kid to hurt. One of my victim's 28-year-old brother showed up at my school one day and called me out from my class. Without saying a word, he punched me right in the chest, sending me flying across the hall. A sharp pain pulsed under my ribs and I couldn't breathe. Convinced I was going to die, I was scared but felt that I deserved it... until the poison that kept me going flooded my veins once again – *anger.* Who was person to undermine my authority and make me look weak? *So much anger.* I only hoped no one saw, picked myself up, and pretended nothing happened.

Unfortunately, this moment of violence would not be the last. For me, violence and drinking went hand in hand. If I drank, I fought ... and I drank a lot. Broken bones, concussions, bruises, cuts – those became my medals of honour, a reminder that I was strong and in control. Regardless of how much I drank, I always came to and remember being surprised that no matter what, my body would wake up. As you can imagine, terrible things happened when I blacked out. I only know because those were the times I woke up in the hospital. I can remember one doctor looking down his nose at me, clearly disgusted at a 14-year-old so out of control, saying 'you have a concussion'. Apparently, I had fallen out of my first-floor apartment window. There was no compassion in his voice, just a statement of the facts. I caught a glimpse of myself this time in the mirror and wept at the image I saw. Like two-face from the Batman comics, half my face was completely disfigured – a bloody, dirty mess. Of course, I had no one to take care of me. In fact, it's a wonder my face healed without any long-lasting scars – I only had alcohol and hydrogen peroxide to keep it clean and didn't really know what I was doing. So young and alone.

My home, if you can call it a *home*, was always full of strangers, coming and going as they pleased. Young guys were flirting with me and old farts would shamelessly hit on me. My parents did nothing to protect me, so I became an easy target. There were times I was drugged in the basement of our apartment and raped. Sometimes, I'd be lucky and have warning that men were on their way. That way I could jump out my window and disappear for a few hours, thankful to escape their torment for the time being. When I had no warning, if the men were in the mood to 'play', I was their readily available victim. This abuse and torture only hardened my heart further. I eventually turned to drugs to ease some of the pain. Although I had few physical scars at the time, my soul was thoroughly marred and there was yet more heartbreak on the way.

Chapter 6

Home Life

———————— ✳ ————————

*W*hen I thought things couldn't get any worse, I woke up one day with severe abdominal pain. Until then, I had never experienced pain so excruciating – like all my bones were breaking and all my muscles were contracting at the same time. I had no fever, so I stayed in bed hoping the pain would just go away. As the day wore on and my pain increased, I could not stay quiet. Eventually my mother responded to my wailing – perhaps the only time I've known an ounce of motherly affection from her. I put my head on her lap and she gently stroked my hair. Despite the pain, I could have stayed in that tender moment forever – finally! My mother's love! But it was over as quick as it had started. She decided I needed a doctor.

Once at the doctor's office, it became apparent that I was actually having labour pains – I was giving birth! I was shocked and confused, waiting for some type of explanation. "You have to be pregnant to have a baby..." I thought hoping this was all a mistake. "You are having a baby" the doctor confirmed. Time froze and I became paralyzed as dread washed over me, then guilt and shame. How could my starving, ema-ciated, and often intoxicated body sustain an innocent little baby without me knowing? I decided to leave the clinic. I wasn't sure where I would go, but this baby could not be born. The doctors stopped me and called an ambulance to take me to the hospital, while my mother stood in the periphery. In that moment I hated her the most I had ever felt. How did she not see this coming? Then the hate turned inwards again, how did *I* not see this coming? I hated myself for not knowing.

My water broke and the pain and fear escalated. I was ready to pass out. I was familiar with the doctor's disgust – I had encountered it many times before, only this time he started to scold my mother. She wasn't having that, so she left. I was alone … again. Defeated I followed their instruc-tions without arguing. Surrounded by strangers, I thought this was the end. My labour was intense, but quick. Within two hours my baby was born. Her tiny pink body was alive, wiggling & making noises. The nurse put her on the table beside me. As I turned to face her, I was again astounded that my abused body was able to carry something so pure, but deep down I knew the alcohol, drugs, and starvation would all have an impact on her health. The pediatrician counted her fingers and toes, all was fine there, but some-thing else was wrong. She said that we should schedule a meeting with the head of the hospital to review our options.

The next day my mother came, and we went to the office for our meeting with the doctors. They looked at us both with judgment and disgust in their eyes. The doctor shamed us for the negligence and gave us a long moral lecture. Then he said that baby has a birth defect. The palate on the roof of the mouth which separates the oral cavity from the nasal cavity, wasn't formed, therefore she wouldn't able to feed and probably wouldn't survive. She would need very close medical attention for as long as she lived. "Don't bring her home," my mother said bluntly. "Who will take care of her? You?" I was numb, having just found out my daughter would most likely die. "If you refuse to take the baby home, we will take care of her for however long she lasts." Gently said one of the nurses. I was devastated and began contemplating if and how I could care for my own baby. They emphasized all the medical attention she would need and it became clear that I would not be able to provide for her. I started crying, repulsed that I turned out to be just like my mother – careless and neglectful. The decision was made for my baby to stay in the hospital, but in order for all paperwork to be completed and everything finalized I had to give her a name, and gave up my parental rights. Ksenia. My sweet, baby Ksenia. She would be 23 years old today.

I can remember the deep sorrow of my time in the hospital very well. Back then, you had to stay in the hospital for 7 days after giving birth. I was in a room with 3 other women who were all enjoying the presence of their newborn. Their joy as they told stories of anticipation and excited family members cut my heart like a knife. Many days I could not stop crying. I knew this pain was something I would have to live with for the rest of my life. But the women were kind to me. They knew I had lost my baby and took pity on me, perhaps one of the only few people in my life so far who did so. They fed me as I had no food and helped wrap my chest to stop my milk from coming in. Such natural nurturers, something I had never experienced from my own mother.

As I've said, all this time I was alone. My grandparents were in the dark. I wanted to spare them this horror. I was so ashamed. I didn't even know who Ksenia's father was! The sexual abuse I suffered was so frequent, it was impossible to know. My agony was crushing. The day came for me to be discharged from the hospital. The other women's families, the 'normal people' I thought to myself, all came. There were flowers, champagne, gifts for the baby, gifts for the doctor... I had no one and nothing. Each woman would leave with their little colour-coded bundle of joy, everyone knew blue was a boy and red was a girl. Not me. I walked out of that hospital empty handed and heartbroken, only to return to an even emptier life. Hours passed while I waited for someone to pick me up... no one came. Eventually, my 8-year-old baby brother showed up. My mother had a huge black eye. She said she got into a fight the night before and that she had a hangover like it was supposed to make me feel better that she didn't show up for me.

Although I left my baby at the hospital, she never left my heart. My friend's mom worked at the hospital and I was able to get updates on Ksenia's progress from her. The updates were never good or hopeful. After three months, Ksenia passed away. I knew it in my heart even before I knew it in my head. Despite not being able to take care of her in life, I was determined to give her a proper burial – I felt I owed her at least that much. I went to the morgue to collect her little lifeless body. My friends were able to get some cash together for me to buy an actual casket, the only dignity I could offer her. I got home and placed the small coffin on our kitchen table. The weight of grief was suffocating. Thankfully, no one was home, and I had this time to myself. I went to the cemetery. My friends helped me dig a hole in the frozen earth. People were getting ready to celebrate New Year's Eve and I was burying my child. I was 15 years old.

Chapter 7

Deeper

The days after losing Ksenia feel like a blur when I try and look back on them. To medicate the pain, I turned to alcohol and drugs. Hours turned into days, turned into months, turned into years and one day I met a boy. He said he would heal the pain he saw deep in my eyes. His parents loved me, and I thought maybe I had a chance at a "normal life" with him. He didn't seem to mind my crazy family and my reputation. Thinking I could settle down and live a normal life, I tried to find a job. I became a vendor at the bazar. It was not a great job – but a job still. Even in the middle of the winter my employer refused to let me stay home. He made me work outside in -30-degree weather. I got pneumonia and was hospitalized. Spending time in the hospital brought back bad memories. No newborn babies and happy mothers this time, instead, I was sharing a room with a crazy lady! She seemed to always be mumbling and I could never understand what she was saying. Definitely crazy, I concluded. One day after one of her mumbling sessions, she explained that she was praying to God in tongues, the language of the holy spirit. I chuckled and concluded she was even crazier than I first thought! She tried to tell me about God, but I didn't care. I knew that if there was a God and a devil fighting for my soul ... the devil was winning.

Once I recovered from having pneumonia, I found out I was pregnant again. By this time, however, I knew I wasn't mother material. I would never have a baby again, I promised myself. So, I went for my first abortion. A procedure I found extremely painful. I was jarred by the contrast of happy nurses chatting about their vacations as they dug around in my uterus. The procedure only lasted 10-15 minutes, but I cried the whole time and took a long time to recover, adding another scar to my soul.

I tried to have a "normal" job, I really did. I quickly realized that at this time in my country, no one under 18 could have a good job and fair pay. I had to find a way to take care of myself, so I started playing cards for money. I love games and love to win, so this was easy money for me. When you get involved in this scene, you meet a lot of sketchy characters. I started hanging out with a gang of women, tough criminals just out of jail. Running with them, I knew I wouldn't be the victim anymore. Smoking, drinking, and doing drugs had always been a part of my life, but with these women, it was next level. Until I had met them, I had never tried any hard drugs. They were always pressuring me to try, assuring me that I was going to love the high, but I was terrified of needles. They finally convinced me it was 'safe' and I agreed. I had never experienced anything like it. Drinking too much always gave me a hangover, but these new drugs just made me feel free – free from worry, fear, hunger, pain. Free from the struggle of living! The word for this euphoria sounds like, "kaif" and the drug we called "shirka". The closest thing would be heroin.

Shirka became my new purpose. It was the reason I woke up in the morning – make money to afford my next hit. Can't make money? Steal something you can sell instead. Any criminal activity I got wind of became an opportunity, from small scale, like stealing bikes, to larger scale like robbing entire stores. The race on this hamster wheel escalated. I was no longer even getting high, just maintaining a new normal. Missing a dose was not an option. My body needed these drugs like it needed water and oxygen.

The constant search for drugs was my life for two years and two years was long enough. I was getting tired of this lifestyle and wanted an escape. I knew my father was living on a farm in the middle of nowhere with his friends. I hated that family but hated my current lifestyle more. My dad owned chickens, cows, and even a horse. This life suited him – he had always loved nature. When I first moved out there, I was sick from the withdrawal but once my dependency on the drugs wore off a bit, I could help my dad around the farm to take my mind off the discomfort in my body. He trained me how to herd cows and although I was terrified, I was after all a city girl, I really enjoyed it! The most important thing is to keep the cows in line with the rest of the herd – they have a tendency to stray and go in the opposite direction you want them to. At times, I felt like we had a lot in common. I never wanted to follow the crowd. I started with the calves because I was so scared of the big cows, but eventually my dad let me drive the big cows, too. My dad used a large stick, on which he engraved 'Tylenol' (at least that's the English translation) He instructed me to smack them right between the horns whenever they didn't obey – a little dose of 'Tylenol'. It was his little joke. For the time being I had everything I could want – a place to stay, freedom to do whatever I wanted, and an opportunity to exercise my control and flex my authority, even if it was just with animals.

I loved the fresh air and solitude out in the country. In evenings I would sit alone on top of a hill and watch the sun set surrounded by nothing but beautiful, quiet, peaceful nature. Sunflower fields and green pastures made my mind soar. In these moments of seclusion, I would feel a hope rising in my soul, an ache for something more, as I became gripped with the knowledge that I was special, that there had to be some purpose for my life. It was something I desperately wanted to be true. Alone in the wilderness I could cry, laugh, or scream. I thought I was talking to myself but now I know in these moments, I was pouring my heart out to a God who was listening when I didn't even believe in him.

This quieter life was just the escape I needed, but I was getting restless. I was "clean" for a few weeks and I was bored. I tried hard to fit in, to be normal, but when you know what it's like to be high it's always on your mind, forever a dormant craving. On hot days, we would drive to a pond across the village to swim. On one of these days as we were making our way through the village we stopped at the store. I stayed in the car and let my eyes wander, taking in the scenery around me. My eyes rested on an abandoned greenhouse. The glass was broken, the metal corroded. My heart filled with sadness as my eyes took in the destruction and weeds, lots and lots of weeds. I couldn't help but see myself in that abandoned greenhouse… trying to survive but get choked by everything around you. My eyes stopped, freezing in place. I couldn't believe what I was seeing. Those weren't just any weeds. It was *weed* … marijuana! Without even thinking, I got out of the car and started collecting the plant so I could dry it and smoke it later. Before I got too excited at the potential before me, I had to determine the quality. I canceled my trip to the pond and rushed home instead. Once the plant was dried, I rolled it and smoked it. The familiar calm washed over me as I inhaled and exhaled. This wasn't just weed, this was *good* weed and good weed means money. Ever the opportunist, I had found my ticket back to the city and another means of survival

Back in the city I was able to sell and cover my rent and food. I was proud for making a life for myself. But the stability didn't last long. Before I knew it, I was addicted to drugs again, hanging around with the same trouble-makers. I was lost, angry, miserable, and only 18 years old. Convinced my life wasn't going anywhere, I almost didn't believe him when he said he had a job for me. Who is this guy who offered me a job? I honestly don't even remember. I was just so happy to be given an opportunity for something different, I didn't care *who* was offering.

Chapter 8

Cairo, Egypt

There were two options for people like me – jail or death. I had seen and known enough people who went one of those two ways and I did not want to end up like them. That quiet voice I heard speaking to me on the hilltops in the countryside whispered again, *you were made for* more. That's why, when this vague offer of a job came to me, I was instantly interested. The mysterious man introduced me to his friend, a very nice and very rich looking woman. This woman brought me to her house and offered me fancy coffee and sweets. I was very impressed. She told me that she would be able to find me a job, no specifics, just *a job*. Without much thought, overwhelmed with the pleasantness of this woman and all her wealth, I accepted eager to escape.

Almost immediately, her 'team' went to work. I was taken to a fancy salon to have my hair done and was dressed in fashion from even fancier stores. Wearing a fur coat and full face of make-up, I started to question what work I would actually be doing and why I had to look so nice – looking back, I understand I was naïve, but what did I know? They gave me a passport and took me to the Israeli embassy. Apparently, I had family in Israel that I hadn't seen in many years and wanted to reconnect. At least, that was the story I was to tell. It seemed my story was not very believable and so I was denied a visa. I left the embassy unaware of the complication this denial would be. This woman and her team were very angry but promised me there was another way. I guess whatever my job was, it was in Israel. Still on heavy drugs, I was unable to sense that something might be wrong, so I played along with whatever they asked me to do.

I vaguely remember the airport – how I got through customs, I'll never know – and the plane ride is even further in my memory. I just know that one day, I woke up hearing the Muslim call to prayer as 'Allahu akbar' rang out. Confused, I tried to ascertain where I was. I looked out the window and saw clementine oranges growing on the trees. For a kid who only saw this fruit at Christmas, this was fascinating. *Where was I?* It was a warm summer day and I quickly realized that my thick jeans, heavy plaid shirt and winter boots were well out of place. I was sweating. Then, as any addict, I started to think about where my next dose was going to come from. I was already nauseous and was going to need it soon. Fear and panic cut into my core. There wasn't going to be a next dose. My withdrawal was bad. For many days, I couldn't eat and was throwing up non-stop. I was weak but remained allured by glimpses of my new surroundings.

I found out that we were in Cairo, Egypt. Despite my withdrawal sickness, I was very excited. I thought, *finally* my dreams are coming true! All my life I was fascinated by Egyptian culture and architecture. Ever since learning about Cleopatra as a kid, I dreamt of seeing Egypt with my own eyes. I could never imagine that one day I would actually have the chance to! Once my withdrawal symptoms became manageable, I was able to tour the city a bit more.

Everything was amazing and more than I ever thought was possible for me. We had two men accompanying us five girls, one of the men acting as our guide. Our story was simple – we were on a class trip! They took us to a beautiful city on the Red Sea where every building was painted white, Sharm el Sheikh. I had never seen anything so exotic in my life. We climbed up a cliff and watched the sun set over the Red Sea. I was mesmerized by the red and orange hues splashed across the vast canvass of sky and ocean, so thankful in my heart that I was given this chance to witness such beauty. We ate Middle Eastern food and enjoyed the culture and music. I even got to walk along the seashore at night and dip my toes in the water. I was in heaven.

The next morning our room was raided by the police and we were all taken to the police station to be questioned and registered. They took our passports, took our fingerprints, and wrote down everything we said. They repeated over and over, "Why are you here?", but we had been given our script and stuck to it. "We are on a class trip..." This went on for hours and I was getting scared. Finally, they let us girls go but kept our guide.

We had no money, no food, and no idea where we were. The second man that was with us had disappeared and the other one was in jail. What were we to do? After some brainstorming, we figured out that we were about 6 hours from Cairo, where we were before Sharm el Sheikh. Someone even remembered the name of our hotel in Cairo – a miracle! We flagged down a taxi and explained our situation in a broken collection of Russian, little bit of English, and even less Arabic. We were lost, had no money, and needed to make it back to Cairo. If he could take us to Cairo, we could pay him at the hotel. I'm not sure why this taxi driver even believed us – perhaps he had his suspicions – but he agreed. He was a kind enough man and stopped to get us food and water. We tore into the provisions like wild animals. After a few hours, we arrived back to our hotel in Cairo. The second man who had disappeared was there, shocked to see us. He had heard we got arrested and assumed we were in jail. He was impressed we found our way back as we joyfully told him of our 'adventure'. He laughed and gave the taxi driver his money. When the taxi driver left, our guide sobered up. "We are off schedule. I'll have to make a call".

In a few hours, we were on the road again headed for another mysterious destination. We crossed the famous Nile, which was just a dark, dirty, green river. I was disappointed, it wasn't the same as in my imagination. In fact, not much was turning out to be what I imagined. It felt like we drove for hours and hours, through desert and sand dunes. Finally, we arrived at a tent in the middle of nowhere. Our guide said goodbye and left us girls with two terrifying Middle Eastern men. The magic was gone and I knew I was in trouble. Watching the man drive away it dawned on me that I had just witnessed the moment I was sold and knew I would be trafficked to another foreign country.

The two men shoved us into the tent. They did not treat us well. At night, hungry and tired, they forced us to walk through the dark, cold desert. Over sand dunes and under barbed wire. We waited silently. I could see soldiers at their post. I could hear them speak, that's how close we were. A few years later, the Egypt-Israel border would be equipped with cameras and motion detectors. A pity it wasn't available when we were crossing, for surely, we would have been caught or wouldn't even have attempted. Crossing the border illegally was dangerous. Fear and uneasy feelings settled among us. It was very cold; the temperature drops in the desert at night very fast. Born and raised in an industrial city, I never saw a night sky like the one in the desert. For a moment I forgot what I was doing and got lost in exploring the beauty of myriad stars above. They were so close I thought I could reach out and touch them! I was jolted from this peaceful escape when were told to crawl back under the wire, back into Egypt. As I said, we were apparently off schedule, and no one was there to receive us.

Hungry and thirsty, we trudged back to the tent in the middle of nowhere. Exhausted and scared, they didn't understand anything we tried to say to them. In exasperation, I finally started yelling at them in Russian, thinking nothing could get any worse than it already was. As I said, I was naïve. A man stormed into the tent, livid that I was causing a scene. He quickly covered the distance between us with long strides and put a gun to my head, swearing at me in Arabic. His face was so close that I could smell the stench of his sweat. His saliva was foaming in the corner of his mouth like a dog with rabies. Feeling the cold weapon against my forehead and seeing this raging animal in front of me, I started to say goodbye to my life. But the pride and adrenalin coursing through my veins, the same pride and adrenaline that kept me safe on the streets in Ukraine, would not allow me to back down. I had no sense of self-worth, no value in being alive, so I had nothing to lose. I guess the man thought I would shut up once I saw the gun, but I figured I was more valuable to him alive - to him I was just a pile of money- so I didn't back down. He stormed out and shouted instructions to the other man, who then brought us water and potato chips. At least my outburst was good for something.

The next day, the men ordered us into the bed of a truck. They threw huge, heavy spare tires on top of us – relishing in our pain – and then covered us with a tarp. We were to try crossing the border again. As we approached the border, we became frozen with fear and remained silent. Through a crack, I saw machine guns and soldiers... it was just a police check before the border. We were cleared to proceed and drove for a while until we were met by other men. We were hurried out of the truck. We ran, crawled under a fence, and ran again. This time, a jeep was waiting for us. It was unreal. At the time, I thought to myself that one day I would write a book. Well, here I am.

Chapter 9

Israel

*O*nce in Israel, we ended up in Tel Aviv. From there, we were separated and sold to different brothels. I heard your life depended on which brothel you ended up in. Some places were brutal where girls would die, never to be seen again. Other places actually gave you a cut of what you earned them. My 'mahon', the Hebrew slang for brothel, turned out to be one of the better ones. They had strict rules and regulations in place to protect us girls from cruelty. Still, I was an object to be used and sold, just another commodity in the marketplace, not much different from the spices and tacky souvenirs sold in the souks.

Most of the girls were Russian. No surprise there. The owners were Jewish but hired Russian bodyguards to communicate with us girls. Some girls had been doctors, nurses, wives, and mothers back home. Some were there 'willingly' so they could work to provide money for their families back home. Poverty always was the mother of necessity, which makes me wonder if it really was a choice. At my brothel, no one else seemed particularly *forced* to be there. In fact, there seemed to be a strange sense of community even. No judgement, no drama ... just women trying to survive as best they can. Some older women tried to take me, the 'child', under their wing, but I made it very clear I needed no one.

I was propelled by my primal instinct to survive. Once I grasped the fact that I was sold into prostitution, I tried to build a life for myself within that harsh reality. The fact was, men wanted my body and I was to give it to them, I had no choice in that, but men also wanted attention, I thought. They were longing for company, yearning to be noticed, desiring to be heard, and looking for 'love'. I used this to my advantage and lured them in with my looks and promise of love. I quickly found ways to manipulate men to get what I wanted. I made them believe I cared. They exploited my body, I, in turn, exploited their loneliness, weakness, and vulnerability. I lived by the philosophy that if anyone wanted to use me, they could be used by me. In this way, I believed I always had the upper hand. I had no boundaries and no limits to my wicked game. I survived the streets of Ukraine, why would I let Israel be any different? Actually, Israel was an improvement – at least I wasn't getting raped and beaten in my own home – and there was money to be made.

Once I saw the potential, my goal was to become rich. I promised myself I would never be hungry again and once the money started coming in, I lavished myself with gold, diamonds, the latest fashions, and all types of delicious foods. I told myself I was finally wanted, finally *needed...* but peace of mind and contentment eluded me. I tried so many things to obtain this state of mind, always convinced that satisfaction was just on the other side of this luxury, that luxury when really all my indulgences left me empty.

I quickly realized money could buy a lot of things, but not peace of mind. Drugs had worked in the past, so I turned to my old friend again. Money, drug dealers and people went through my hands like sand. Once again, drugs provided an escape, enabling me to turn off any pangs of guilt and shame that threatened to destroy this new life I had created. My life became all about me – my pleasure, my comfort, my survival. I was the only object of my love and worship.

Chapter 10

Praying for a Miracle

$\mathcal{B}$ ack home, my grandma didn't even know what was going on with me. I loved her too much to inflict on her the pain of embarrassment and disappointment for my new life. I lied to her about what I was doing in Israel, I lied to everyone. I had a carefully crafted story prepared to answer all her questions. I pretended that I had a normal life, a normal job, and a wonderful boyfriend so there was nothing to worry about. She believed me and was so happy for me! I called her often. "Everything is the same. Don't worry about us. We are all together here, but you are alone. You take care of yourself, and we'll be fine." Was her favorite response. I knew this was a lie, too. Something was always going on, but she always tried to shelter me from bad news.

As a child, I always had difficulty sleeping, but in Israel I didn't seem to have a problem – I was finally sleeping through the night and even having dreams, some very vivid. One dream scared me. I was back home at my grandma's apartment. I stood in the hallway alone in silence. I was looking around with a deep sense of fear. It was so gray and damp and empty. No furniture no carpets and no wallpaper except one mirror on the wall covered with black cloth. In my country, this means someone has died. They believe that evil spirits and demons come to visit family in mourning through these mirrors. I was astonished and frozen unable to move. Then in the corner of my eye I saw light shining from under the kitchen door. The door swung open and my grandma was delighted to see me. I looked past her and saw all the women of my family gathered to cook a feast together; soup being prepared to feed guests after the burial. There was no man present. "Where is my grandpa?" I asked and my heart start pounding hard. I woke up.

I called home and my grandma answered in a cheerful voice. No hello from me, I demanded to know where my grandpa was. My grandma responded with shock, "How did you know? Who told you?" she was upset. At once, I just *knew* ... my scary dream was almost reality. My grandpa had had a massive stroke and was in critical condition in the hospital. I was gathering my thoughts on the other end and she was silent as well. She broke the silence by telling me that the doctors were doing everything they could, but that it's in the hands of God. It's funny how some people who don't even believe in God refer to his omnipotence when they feel out of control. The doctors told my grandma that she needed a miracle.

I just knew that if my grandpa were to die, my grandma would follow shortly after. They went through everything in life together – the good and the bad – true love! I couldn't lose them both and my mind started cycling through the familiar waves of panic and fear. A word came into my mind 'Kotel' and I brushed it aside. I hung up the phone with grandma and was intent on figuring out to get my grandma a miracle.

My brothel hired a man named Alex to keep us safe. He was a Christian and often told us girls Bible stories in ways we had never heard before. He was so sure that God was real and present in his life that it got my attention. I had never met anyone like this before. Such joy and delight on his face whenever he spoke about Jesus. He told me about him and his family's struggles. They were persecuted for following Jesus and so fled to Tel Aviv, where he felt like they were called to be. He openly shared the Gospel with everyone, and nobody seemed to mind. He gave me my first Bible, a kid's Bible with pictures in it. He knew I probably wouldn't read it (I didn't...), but I would fan through the pages once in a while. Those pictures spoke a thousand words and a seed was planted. In one of our conversations, Alex told me about an ancient wall in Jerusalem that was built thousands of years ago. It was considered holy ground and was known as the Western Wall, the Wailing Wall, or simply as Kotel. He said whenever he needed a supernatural intervention in whatever was happening, he would go there, and God seemed to answer his prayers. My eyes lit up at the possibilities, at the time all for material things. "You can't ask for a Ferrari" he warned, "God is not a genie granting wishes from a lamp..."

After the phone call with my grandma, I remembered this conversation and understood why the word 'Kotel' came into my mind while on the phone. The fear for my grandpa's life was weighing heavily on me. I felt a strong desire to go to Jerusalem to the Wailing Wall and ask Alex's God for a miracle. I believed only this God could save him. I called every bus and taxi company only to get rejected from each and every one. A terrorist had attacked the highway, so tourism was on hold. The only way to Jerusalem now was a long drive through the valley, and no wanted to risk their life just for me. Exasperated, I yelled "How can I ask for a miracle if no one wants to drive me there!?"

That same day Alex called me and said "I have a strong feeling that God is asking me to go to Jerusalem. Would you like to join us? I will show you around and we will visit the Wailing Wall." I knew this was a miracle in itself. I was ready to pay tons of money to go there alone and yet God provided a safe, free ride with good company.. "YES, YES! I'm coming!" I couldn't contain my excitement. When he came to pick me up, he was with his young daughter. I asked why he was bringing his daughter on such a dangerous journey, but he simply replied that God would protect us.

It was a beautiful ride. I saw many historical places and didn't even know it. I walked where Jesus walked, before I even knew who Jesus was. Looking back, I always marvel at how God chose Israel to be the place we would meet. During this car ride, I felt a faith welling up inside me. God would answer my prayers. Suddenly, a loud pop rang out, and Alex lost control of the car. Seeing as how a bus was just attacked by terrorists a few days ago on this very road, I assumed it was a bomb. Alex wrestled control of the car and we came to a stop. Just a blown tire. Another miracle – we survived. Alex was puzzled, his tires were new. Most people in this moment would be in distress, not Alex. He confidently got out of the car praising God for keeping us safe and began to *joyfully* replace the tire. What strange behavior, I thought, but this joy was infectious. I started to thank God in my own heart as I began to see God's hand in this journey. Tire replaced, we were on our way without any further delays.

Chapter 11

Jerusalem

*J*erusalem! Beautiful, mysterious, unique... I couldn't get enough of its original architecture and ancient history. The sights, smells and sounds of the city were just like I had read in books as a kid. My inner explorer was bursting with exhilaration. Alex's daughter, though only 9 or 10 at the time, proudly announced the significance of each place we visited, the best guide you could wish for. They were here often. I admired this little girl's knowledge and was fascinated that this kid had so much passion for this city and for God. While I was enthralled with everything we saw, my mission was Kotel and finally we were there.

The sight was astonishing. I had never seen so many people amassed in one place. I got very tense. At that moment his daughter slid her little hand into mine. "Don't worry I will take care of you" she smiled sweetly. Alex could not accompany us because the men and women pray separately. I confessed that I didn't know what to do. The little girl explained that you could borrow some scriptures from a library in any language you require, you just have to return them. It was also important that you do not turn your back to the wall. "When you are done, you slowly walk backwards facing the Wall until you get to this point" she pointed to the ground, patiently instructing me like a mature professor. She continued explaining the rest of the formalities, but my mind was a blur. Before I knew it, we were walking towards the wall. Woman of all ages and nationalities united in a sea of murmured chants, wailing their prayers in all different languages.

Before today, I hadn't really considered what my experience was going to be like. I had a sliver of faith that I would encounter God in some way, but no set of expectations about what it would look and feel like. The closer we inched towards the wall, my mind went to darker and darker places of my soul. Who was I to approach this 'holy ground'? I wasn't worthy of this audience. All my dark deeds flashed before my eyes and I was overcome with a deep sense of shame. People like me don't deserve any mercy, besides I didn't even know *how* to pray.

The line filed forward, and I was finally facing the wall all alone, just like I had been my entire life. A little bit dazed at the gravity of the moment, I looked from side to side hoping to take a cue on how to proceed. I saw that all women had their eyes closed as they pleaded with God, some crying, some silent with the trembling of their lips barely visible, and others intensely whispering. Everyone seemed to be rocking back and forth as they prayed, with their hands on the wall. The voices seemed to get louder, and I was getting hotter. I was suddenly very aware of my thirst. I look back at this memory with new understanding. There's a passage in scripture where Jesus stops at a well and starts a conversation with a woman by asking her for some water. It's a poignant passage as the woman was of a different religion and was shocked to be spoken to by a Jewish man. Confused, she tries to understand who this man was:

> *Jesus replied, "Anyone who drinks this water will soon become thirsty again. But those who drink the water I give will never be thirsty again. It becomes a fresh, bubbling spring within them, giving them eternal life.*
>
> *John 4:13-14.*

I felt weak from the sun and the heavy burden of shame in my soul. My mind was busy, my heart even heavier. I looked at the Wall and placed my palms on the smooth, ancient surface. Leaning forward I realized that the stone was cool to the touch. A peace came over me instantly. My shaky voice started, "God... please forgive me... I don't know how to pray... I am sorry that my life is a mess... Please help... Save my grandpa from death..." and words start pouring out of my mouth. It was surreal. Like a gushing river, I couldn't stop. I was reminded of the 'crazy' lady I shared a hospital room with many years ago, she didn't seem so crazy anymore. When I was done and opened my eyes, I realized that my face, my neck, and my shirt were covered with tears. My body was trembling, but my mind was calm. I felt respect and gratitude to God that He allowed me to be in His presence. I 'knew" everything was going to be ok. I moved backwards slowly, remembering the little girl's instructions, and basked in the intensity of emotion so that it would be imprinted on my memory forever. I had never experienced peace like this before.

I found my little friend. She was sitting on the curb of the road beside some old ladies with buckets of red string bracelets. I got one as a reminder of this event. I told her that I had just had the best experience of my entire life and she looked at me, "You were there for over an hour!". I couldn't believe it, but the seriousness of her look made me believe. We left the area to reconnect with Alex. Shortly after, I called home. My grandpa had been healed.

Chapter 12

Rising Tensions

*O*ver time, I had fallen in love with Israel. I had really loved it from day one. The flora and fauna were completely different to anything back home and they had warm weather for six months in a row. Then, the rainy season. I never saw anything like this! Rain drops- huge blasts of water from an angry sky, fast becoming a flood on the ground. Thunder so loud and powerful that I thought the glass of my windows would shatter. Sounds, more like explosions, of the tropical storms would send fear into my spine.

I loved to take walks as the range of exotic flowers captivated me with their rich colours and alluring scent. I've mentioned before the clementines, but this really amazed me! That rare fruit was a special treat only on Christmas. Here, they were literally falling from the trees. All the fruits and vegetables had a sumptuous freshness to them. Bananas and kiwis, which I hated before because they were never ripe back home, became my favorite fruits.

The people looked so different as well. Boys had gel and spiked their hair, girls had tattoos and piercings and different hair colours. Ukraine at the time was very conservative. Only people who went to prison had tattoos, so it was a shock to see so many 'normal' people expressing themselves in this way. I felt like this was a place I could fit in.

With the beauty of this country came the sadness as well. I never in my life saw so many solders with guns casually walking on the street. Ukraine was rough, to be sure, but not militarized. At any moment you could be stopped and searched, and you must have your ID anywhere you go. Everyone had military training. Everyone must have 3 years army training and at any time could be called to serve. The cultural tension ran deep and showed it's ugly face daily. One of my friends said the army wouldn't take him because he was the only son left to take care of his mother. Another friend told me he would be willing to die if he could only take two Arabs with him. I know the regional conflict is complex and spans centuries, but I couldn't understand this mind set. "My grandfather hated them, my dad hated them, so I do too..." For him, it was as simple as that. I suppose on some level, I could relate – hate had fueled much of my life – but it pained me to see it operating in so many other lives as well.

Although I was brought to this country against my will, my fondness for it grew and I stayed because I chose to. I was even planning to stay here forever. I often thought about my experience at the Wailing Wall. It wasn't enough to make me change my ways, but I was curious. Something was planted in my heart that day that wouldn't come to fruition for many more years yet. Tensions in the country increased. A new president was elected who wanted to seek peace to the conflict. New laws were created, resolution seemed possible. All that positive momentum changed the day a suicide bomber killed 22 people at a seaside resort. I went the next day and was horrified. Blood soaked asphalt, flowers and candles everywhere contrasted with laughing families frolicking in the sea. How could people carry on so casually? Then I remembered that bomb threats were normal events and how constant vigilance was drilled into everyone. Kids were taught never to accept packages or toys from strangers. Any bag left unsupervised was always suspicious. The threat of death was everywhere. Suddenly I didn't want to be here.

My grandma was worried as she saw tanks on TV and wanted me to come home. I always convinced her I was safe, even though deep down I was looking for a way to get out. I was undecided about whether I would actually leave until one day I went to the mall to buy new shoes. I stepped into the store and a few minutes later police and soldiers stormed the place, ordering me in Hebrew to get out. I froze – all knowledge of my Hebrew vanishing in my panic- and had to be dragged out of the store. There was a bomb inside. Once at a safe distance, I watched on with all the other anxious relatives and friends of people still inside. Thankfully, the bomb didn't go off that day, but I had nightmare that it did. I awoke in a sweaty panic and decided I couldn't stay any longer. That morning I woke up and bought a ticket a home. I wasn't being held captive by my brothel and took the chance to escape when I could. I left behind all my valuables – someone lied to me and told me it would be confiscated at the border anyway – and never looked back. It would be the last time I would be in Israel. Shortly after, 9/11 happened and borders were closed.

Chapter 13

Back in Ukraine

*C*oming home to Ukraine was a strange junction in my life. I didn't know how to integrate my experience in Israel with my life in Ukraine. In my mind, there would be a big reunion with my family who would be excited to welcome me home with open arms. They were happy to see me, sure, but their excitement lasted exactly three days. After that, we slipped into the usual patterns of relating and things were back to normal. With my family indifferent to my return, I began to contemplate what kind of life I was going to live now that I was back. I wanted to be free, to be independent, to achieve something! I didn't want to work in a factory for 30 years, marry 3 times, and have a bunch of children depending on me! Some people could settle for that life, but not me. I always wanted more. Some part of me must have known I wouldn't stay in Israel forever because any money I didn't spend there, I would send home – always one foot in Israel and one in Ukraine. I always hoped that my work in Israel was at least securing a better future for myself. Sending money home turned out to be foolish. I had trusted my aunt to receive the money and put it into an account for me. She received it alright, but then spent it all. Betrayed again, I was shocked that my brothel in Israel had shown me more loyalty than one of my own family members. Back at square one with no money to my name and no chance of returning to Israel, I felt hopeless. Gradually I started to notice how dirty and forlorn my city looked. Growing up you get used to the dreary concrete and factory lined streets and you don't notice it. But having Israel's sunsoaked, cobble-stoned streets fresh in my memory highlighted just how dismal my city was. It didn't take long for me to slip back into my old lifestyle like an old, comfy pair of jeans.

The gangs, drugs, and violence were all too ready to welcome me back. However, my experience at the Wailing Wall had changed me. I was back to my old, familiar ways but I could never shake the feeling that I was being pursued by this God I had encountered at the wall.. How could I forget? For starters, my grandpa was still alive! Every time I looked at him I was reminded of my time at the Wailing Wall. His healing was so complete that he didn't even have any lasting health complications, which is very rare in stroke victims. It was almost as if he never even had a stroke. The doctors and everyone were curious, but I knew who had saved him – God!

"The LORD has heard my plea: the LORD accepts my prayer."
Psalm 6:9 ESV

To mark my grandpa's miracle and show my gratitude to God, I started praying before meals. It was my little way to honour God and give a little back, I thought. My family obviously found it very strange but not my grandpa. I noticed he was wearing a cross around his neck. When I asked him about it, he said that God had saved him! It took a lot for my grandpa to admit that, but I never did tell him that I prayed for him at the wall. I was still trying to figure out what I even believed for myself. Besides, my family wanted nothing to do with God or Jesus. This little flame of belief would be smothered in the days to come. My home environment was so toxic and drugs were all too easy a solution.

In addition to my meal time prayers, I seemed to be meeting more Christians, or at least I was more open to speaking them... maybe they were always around, but I never paid any attention. After coming home, I reconnected with some friends from my teen years. We'd often get into trouble and do drugs together. When we met, I saw that they were clean. Turned out they had become Christians! Their parties without alcohol or drugs were strange at first, but I came to enjoy the innocent fun we always had. We ate good food, which the boys would often prepare and clean up (not very typical for my culture!) and had great conversation. One day they invited me to their church. It was very different from the orthodox churches I had been exposed to growing up. The service I went to had many people that were praying and crying – not unlike my experience the Wailing Wall. From this, I gathered that only people who were desperate came to God, that you must have some huge painful burden. The main orthodox church in our city was built to be more like a tourist attraction, I always thought. So perfectly manicured and sanitized, with artwork on the walls and gold everywhere, it all just seemed like a money grab, a scam. I had always refused to participate in orthodox rituals. How could praying to a bunch of dead saints do anything for me? The smell of the candles and incense always gave me a terrible headache and the 'blessings' never seemed genuine. They were always given in an old Russian vernacular or Latin – how do I know if I was really being blessed and not cursed? But something seemed genuine at my friends' church. It definitely wasn't a money grab – nothing was very fancy here – but people were sincerely seeking, reaching out to a Jesus as though he were alive and accessible! I thought for once this could be the place where I would turn my life around.

Chapter 14

Swallowed Again

———✳———

*U*nfortunately, those Christian friends weren't the only friends I would reconnect with. Another one of my old friends had made quite a name for himself in my absence. He became one of the top drug dealers in the city. Previously I have mentioned shirka – it was the drug we all took and the closest thing to it is heroin. Well, technically it is heroin ... just cut with chemicals to make the high a little different and processing a little cheaper. My friend, a former businessman, saw the opportunity as demand increased. He quit his legitimate endeavours and became engulfed in the illegal production and sale of shirka. He made tons of money, but in the process lost his wife and son to divorce. I was sad to hear this since I had been at their wedding. They were great together ... but, as business partners, so were we. Not long after our reconnection, he exposed me to his whole operation and brought me into the fold. I distance myself from my Christian friends and immersed myself in this new 'business partnership'.

I was glad for the opportunity to be part of something again, something that paid well and gave me the authority I always craved. I acted as the logistics coordinator for this sick, well-oiled machine arranging meetings and collecting money. I was blind to the damage I was doing to people's lives – I was only concerned about taking care of me, living in the now. As ever, my little voice was telling me I wasn't created for me, but a hit of shirka quickly silenced that already frail voice, and I would carry on with my duties.

There are always consequences to drug use, if not immediately, they always catch up with you. My business partner became a junkie before my very eyes. I always despised weak men and to me, his dependence on shirka, was just despicable. He started missing meetings and deliveries. Money was owed. People were looking for him. From all sides, I felt threatened and pressured. My friend got shot, another died of an overdose, and the cops almost beat another friend to death. This was a wake-up call to me.

I remembered my Christian friends and turned to them for help. I wanted to reclaim my life and they agreed to help. By this point, I was well versed in my withdrawal pattern, so I simply gritted my teeth and went through it … again. Once clean, I decided to get a legitimate job. The only thing available was a vendor at a booth in our local market. Working for "crumbs", after thousands went through my hands, was painful. I hated that someone could boss me around. I met a young boy who was part of small gang of kids. He was homeless. I knew he was a thief because a while ago I was just like him. I fed him my lunch and asked about his parents. His dad was gone, and his mother was sleeping in the basement of some building drunk, homeless, with his younger brother. He said he liked to sniff glue to get high. I knew with sadness he wouldn't make it to 15. But it was the best he could do with his situation. There was no hope and no one cared. I hated my job, hated my country, and hated my life. In a few days, I quit and made plans to leave Ukraine for the second time.

Chapter 15

Canada

*W*hile playing a role in my friend's drug enterprise, I had met a girl and moved in with her. As things fell apart with the business, I confided in her that I needed to escape because I was getting worried for my safety. Together, my girlfriend and I, we made plans to leave. My experience in getting to Israel taught me that there are always ways you can get into a country, even countries that are far away and seem *safe*. I reconnected with the same people who got me to Israel, but since that wasn't an option since 9/11, they told me they could get me to Canada instead. The understanding was that I'd be a prostitute, so I'd have to be very careful. My situation in Ukraine was so desperate, I was willing to take the chance.

We arrived on Christmas day and were dropped off at house and told to stay in the basement. The homeowners were Russians, like my traffickers, but they didn't know who we were or anything about our situation. In retrospect, they must have had their suspicions, just like the Egyptian taxi driver who rescued us girls from the dessert, but they never said anything. We lived in this basement for months and we kept our secret for fear that we'd get caught and be deported. Eventually, the traffickers paid some lawyers to get us registered as refugees so that we'd at least be in the country legally. Once you're in Canada legally, you can apply for health cards, work permits, and eventually start your citizenship. Once I knew that I was legal, I began devising a plan to escape which began with convincing my traffickers to let me go to school to learn English.

Miraculously, they agreed to let me sign up for English courses. I knew it'd be the only way I was going to succeed in this new country, so I was eager to go as often as I could. And so I lived my life - school by day, work by night. My girlfriend didn't share my enthusiasm. She had no desire to learn English and Canada's customs. I thought it was dumb. We started to argue a lot. She was comfortable to limit herself by staying in the Russian area and to follow the orders of the people we were staying with. I wanted more. I wanted freedom. I knew I had an opportunity and, thanks to my work and study permits, a means to pursue this opportunity. I started at level zero for English, so required additional support to develop my reading, writing, listening, and speaking skills. I rode the bus 40 minutes each day, careful not to stray from my familiar path.

Talking to strangers was always terrifying, but one day I got lost and didn't have a choice. For a while, I stood there waiting for the right looking person to ask, someone who might be kind enough to bear with my broken English. I finally stopped a lady and she told me to take the subway to where I was going. Annoyed by her advice, I walked away – how dare this woman mock me and tell me to eat at Subway!

I didn't need a sandwich, I need help! I decided to go to the mall until I could figure out where to go. On my way, I saw a huge sign that said 'SUBWAY' with a train on it. Back home, we call this the metro and I realized my mistake. The lady was trying to tell me how to get to the metro so I could take the train! I laughed and I laughed. Eventually, I knew my way around and didn't need as much help navigating this new city, although I always kept written directions in my bag! Even though I was getting better at navigating, there were still days where I would look up and realize I didn't really know where I was. One of those days, I ended up at the lakeshore – I didn't even know my new city had this huge lake! That day I had gotten so lost that I had to use a payphone to call someone and ask for directions.

This fear of the unknown and never feeling familiar inspired me to learn and try to fit in. My ESL teacher was great at helping me assimilate. He had so much passion and even more patience; he truly wanted us to succeed. We were like a junior kindergarten class but with old people. He drew pictures and made faces and he talked super slow. Most of the lessons were role-playing. We learned about different situations we might encounter outside, but I never participated in those lessons. I had a bit of a pride issue. Back home, my test scores had always been really high and my Russian perfect. Here, I felt dumb. I couldn't remember the letters, let alone full words, and my accent was awful. It undermined my confidence. Learning Hebrew was so easy compared to this, the structure was very similar to Russian. I could think in Russian and still produce Hebrew sentences. If I tried that for English, it was a mess! I had to learn to start thinking in English. My Russian friends all assured me that I was wasting my time, that I could get by in broken English for the rest of my life. I was so frustrated that I was the only one who saw the benefit of speaking English. I persevered.

One day the teacher asked me to come to the front of class to perform a dialogue about shopping. I politely declined, but he wouldn't take no for an answer. '"You can do it!", he encouraged me "Just practice, no need for perfection!". Soon he had the whole class chanting my name, "Lena! Lena! Lena!". My face was burning with embarrassment, but I agreed. Shaking like a leaf, I was able to complete the dialogue and sit down. My class applauded... maybe I wasn't as bad as I thought. After this day, I started volunteering more often as I saw the benefit. I learned to laugh at my mistakes and embrace the fact that all of our English was terrible, but that we were all learning together. My classmates became my friends and unlike my Russian "friends" they believed in me and encouraged me. The more I hung out with my classmates, the more my girlfriend got jealous. She hated my progress and didn't like that I had made new friends. After a drunken fist fight, I left her and moved in with another girl. Like in the past, I only exchanged one hell for another.

Chapter 16

Fighting to Survive... Again

———— ✳ ————

*T*he first time I saw her eyes I knew it... it was so familiar. I was into drugs long enough to recognize it anywhere. The desire to get high always overpowers common sense. I had no defense; once a drug addict, always a drug addict I thought. I bluntly asked what she was on. That was the day I tried cocaine for the first time. It was unlike anything I tried before. So began another wild ride! She was exited that I could keep up with her indulgence. She was Canadian and for the first time I was able to see more of this beautiful city. After the drunken the fight with my girlfriend, this other girl welcomed me with open arms. The day I moved out, I got a phone call from my trafficker. He told me I owed them $10,000 and that if I didn't come back, they would hunt me down. I felt a cold shiver down my spine and my mouth got dry with fear and panic. I hung up and threw out my phone. I was angry with myself because I let fear settle in and rest deep in my mind. I couldn't shake the feeling that someone was always watching me. I knew that they couldn't harm me in public and I finally spoke enough English that I could call for help if I needed to. I learned a few emergency phrases just in case. My new girlfriend told me that here in Canada I have rights, that I didn't have to be afraid. I was emboldened by this thought and stayed with this girl.

I liked her home. It was fashionably furnished with leather couches and expensive carpets. She told me that she was a mistress of a wealthy American businessman. "I don't care about money." she said, "I work for fun". She was a dominatrix and spent her time 'enslaving' human beings, but not me – she gave me the freedom to be myself. We spent our nights laughing, talking, drinking, smoking and doing drugs... lots and lots of drugs. I discovered how lonely and sad her life was. We were all suffering, trying to find a way to cope with our pain and misery. Hours became days and days became weeks, I couldn't tell sunsets from sunrises. In the first month we lived together we spent $30,000 on drugs, cigarettes, and booze. Crazy to think that that amount of money is a down payment for a house and some people spend half of their life working to save that amount... we blew it all in one month and it was a joke to us.

After 3 months on this wild ride, I was done. I was bored, sick, and exhausted. I was starting to feel the physical consequences of my hard drug use and it scared me. My nose would often bleed and I had trouble breathing. I told my girlfriend that I wanted to change. "If you want the life of every other loser in this country, the door is open ..." she shot back. It was obvious I didn't really matter to her, she was just afraid to be alone again. Although I left her, I kept her drug dealer. From cocaine, I went to opium, from opium to crack... I was caged by this pattern of addiction. Each time I said it would be different, but I always just exchanged poison for poison.

Although I was pretty much at rock bottom, I loved myself enough not to roll over and die; I refused to accept this fate. My small voice reminding me again and again that I was made for so much more. All I needed was a safe place to stay where I could get clean. I reached out to some "friends", but I quickly learned that one of the side effects of my lifestyle was shallow relationships. No one cared to help. Drugs? They could give me drugs, but nothing beyond that. I was alone and homeless in a foreign country with no one to turn to.

Chapter 17

Tom

I knew a Chinese guy – just an acquaintance. He handled my taxes and would help immigrants by answering questions they had about the government and the legal process of settling in Canada. He once told me he saw a light in me, that I was better than the life I was living. I scoffed at him angrily, "Who do you think you are to judge me?" my paranoia taking over. He got upset, assuming I was being racist. "I don't care who you are! I don't listen to anybody, I make my own rules and live my own life!" I boasted. It felt good to put this man in his place. But when I had no one else to turn to, I remembered him.

I called him up, explained my situation, and asked for money so that I could pay rent. I promised all I needed was one month and that I was good for it. It wasn't too much, I thought, and was confident he would help a girl like me out. He refused. Anger welled up in me, "What about all that junk about seeing light in me?" He interrupted, " I won't give you money ... but I will meet with you and talk". I had no other options, so I agreed.

We met up and Tom brought me a plan of action to get clean and straighten up. "If you have no where to live, there are shelters..." he started. "Are you crazy? I'm not going to live with homeless people", I said in denial. "Well, you are homeless... aren't you?" he quickly replied. Touche. He held the mirror to my situation, and I didn't like what I saw – this really was a new low for me. I always envisioned shelters to be tiny rooms crowded with tons of unwashed people and their ragged belongings... the last place I would turn. On the other hand, I was very stubborn and would do anything to survive. "Give me the number – I'll call them", I replied.

The lady who answered the phone was very kind. I explained my situation and she explained how everything worked. We set an appointment and she gave me an orientation. To my surprise, it was very spacious and clean. They provided food, bus tokens and even had *rules*! I had to show up every day before 9pm in order to get a bed and had to leave again in the morning. Girls stayed separate from the boys and there was no sex or drugs allowed. I felt a glimmer of hope again. Still, the first week was tough as I started experiencing withdrawals. In retrospect, this may have kept me safe from anyone interested in hitting on me. Shelters are notorious for that. Cute, well-dressed, put together girls were easy targets. I looked like a rabid dog and felt even worse. Anyone who tried to approach me, I would curse out. After a week, I was pretty much left alone.

When my withdrawal symptoms weren't too severe, I had a chance to observe the behavior of my shelter mates. I was curious what made them to choose to be here, especially the young, healthy kids. When I felt comfortable enough, I chose a group of young people who accepted me. We easily fell into a routine together – park, library, shelter, park, library, shelter. On our walks I'd share bits of my story, hoping they'd open up and explain their stories too. Most of them thought it was cool just to rebel – they hated their parent's rules and wanted to live life on their own terms, just to aggravate their parents. Others came from more tragic backgrounds. All had quit school, had no job, no dreams, and no discernable future. I could sympathize with my friends who suffered tragic circumstances, but the ones doing this for fun? I was disgusted. They had so much opportunity and were throwing it all away. In Ukraine, no one chose to be on the streets because you would die! There was no government assistance for you, no clean shelter to sleep in at night, no food, no bus tokens … there was nothing! These kids didn't know how good they had it. They had an illusion of freedom but were blinded by pride and rebellion. I saw through it all and knew they weren't free at all. They had no choice about what they could eat, their clothes were only what someone else donated, you can't go wherever you want when you don't have money, and you're sleeping in a different bed every night! I would seethe with jealousy at the thought and rage against the injustice of it all.

I compared myself to my new friends and knew I wasn't like them. I had a different mindset. I was never satisfied with what is, I wanted more… to learn, to grow, to achieve something, to be someone! I changed my swamp for the river dreaming one day to be part of the ocean always hoping it would be enough. I wanted life, I wanted all of it.

But I had Tom. He would check in on me, often taking me to McDonalds for lunch. We were a strange pair. Completely opposite. Most of the time we bickered like an old married couple. I said party he said study. I said expensive he said cheap. I am loud he is quiet. Sometimes people would ask, "Is this old guy your father?" "No! He is my grandmother!" I would chuckle back. He taught me to do laundry and how to set the table. Showed me table manners and taught me to use utensils and chopsticks. He always encouraged me, reminded me that being a newcomer is hard. He often said this with a hint of sadness, as he reflected on his own difficult past. There is pain there. I know he faced lots of discrimination when he came to Canada.

I don't know why he accepted me and all of my crazy. Perhaps it was because I didn't care about the colour of his skin and didn't mind his broken English. He treated me like family and won me over. I had never been treated this way in my life before with such acceptance, warmth, and genuine care. Because of him, I was open to learning even more about 'normal' life behaviors. I must admit my upbringing and lifestyle had left me socially unfit… I knew how to survive, but not thrive. I had much to learn about being a responsible and healthy adult and Tom was there every step of the way. We became best friends. Years later, he walked me down the aisle at my wedding and gave me away. My kids call him 'Uncle Tom' and he's at all our family events. I thank God he brought Tom into my life. I shudder to think where I'd be without him.

Chapter 18

Beginning to Dream

As I've said, Tom was my first role model. He not only showed me how to be a responsible adult, he also showed me the importance of developing skills and talents. All my life, I knew I had potential to be something great, but I never had anyone walking alongside me encouraging me along the way. Tom was my encourager, cheering me on. Once my life seemed to stabilize, he began asking me what I wanted to do with my life. I was always a little annoyed with this question – as if I had a choice! I had no money to do anything, even if I knew what it was that I wanted. Tom was relentless though and never dropped the subject. He could see how discouraged I was by having no money, so he offered to help me find scholarships for whatever it was I wanted to pursue. "Well ..." I quietly answered one day, "I've always wanted to do something creative. I love art, design, fashion... colours and patterns always captivate me..." the wheels in my head were turning. I began to dream, finally having reason to hope my dreams would become a reality with Tom by my side. "I want to be a hairstylist!" I finally declared. Pensively, Tom replied, "Okay, let's see what I can do…", but I knew that in Tom-speak that meant "I'll do everything to make this happen." That was and is one of my favourite things about Tom. Once he agreed to help, he always kept his word with no expectation of anything in return.

Tom helped me get my first job at Canada's Wonderland, showed me how to get food from a food bank, and lastly helped me enroll in a government welfare program. I was finally able to rent a furnished room in a house. I felt accomplished being able to pay rent, but that pride seemed to vanish as soon as my stomach would growl – a cruel reminder that I still needed money for food. Having no spare money for food, I sat on my bed feeling sorry for myself reflecting on my meager existence. There was a soft knock at my door. Through tears, I answered. It was Tom. "I know you spent all your money on rent. I'm so proud of you! Let me buy you some food and bus tokens so you can get around." I cried that day, and I'm crying even now as I write this. No one has ever been so kind to me. He continued to show concern in all areas of my life. He drew me maps, repeated things over and over so I would never get lost. He showed me how to dress professionally and appropriately for different situations. He pushed me to practice my English, correcting not only my grammar but my tone and delivery. Day by day Tom was softening my rough edges, teaching me to trust, and helping me reestablish a firm foundation for my life. He was the best parent I never had, celebrating my achievements as though they were his own.

True to his word, Tom found a cosmetology school that I could apply to. With some government funding and diligent budgeting, I would be able to afford a one year course. Although it was just the beginning of summer and the program didn't start until September, I went to apply in person ... with Tom, of course. I greeted the receptionist and proudly declared I would like to apply. Unimpressed, she asked what my English level was. My accent was betraying me. "You need to be at least a level 6 if you are going to be able to follow the assignments and write the final exam." For a moment, I was stuck in shame – my English was only level 4- but I went from shame to angry. Inside I was burning with rage, "How dare this woman tell me what I can and cannot do!" I thought to myself. But, thinking of Tom and everything he did to get me here, I sweetly replied " Yes, I'm aware. Please put my name on the list for this course." She gave me the paperwork with a chuckle, sure she would never see me again. I left that day feeling energized. For the first time in my life, I had a goal beyond surviving.

That summer I studied more than all my school years combined. My commute to Canada's Wonderland was over an hour, so I used this time to my advantage. I took out simple books from the library and slowly moved up to novels. I always had a dictionary on me – long before the time of iPhones – and constantly had to look up words I didn't know. Each bus ride, each dictionary entry, brought me closer to my goal. There were times I felt discouraged, but I would repeat to myself, "I am smart. I am clever. I am bright. I am happy. I am lucky. I am rich. I am Canadian. Everything is possible!". These affirmation statements carried me through and eventually the summer came to an end.

Chapter 19

Dreams Come True

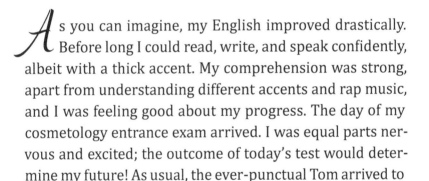

*A*s you can imagine, my English improved drastically. Before long I could read, write, and speak confidently, albeit with a thick accent. My comprehension was strong, apart from understanding different accents and rap music, and I was feeling good about my progress. The day of my cosmetology entrance exam arrived. I was equal parts nervous and excited; the outcome of today's test would determine my future! As usual, the ever-punctual Tom arrived to accompany to my test. It was a chilly September morning, yet the atmosphere at school was boiling with anticipation.

We were led to a gymnasium and arranged in rows. Heart pounding, I took my seat glancing around at my fellow test takers. "oh, I hate math ... we're starting with math! What if I fail because there's math?" my internal dialogue turned against me. I began falling apart, thinking of how high the stakes were. Then, I remembered the affirmation statements I would repeat to myself all summer long and I replaced my negative self-talk. With that, I banished the question of 'what if...'. Instead, I would just focus on the test. Before long, my math portion was finished – easy! The next portion was a written essay. I chose to write about one of my neighbours, an exchange student from Mexico that had recently returned to her home. She was the first person I ever opened up to about my entire past and she listened without judgement. I loved her deeply so had no problem writing an entire essay about her. I began pouring my heart onto the page with as much English as I knew. After a while, I forgot about the mark and continued to write just because it felt so good to put my thoughts on a page. A foreshadow to the process of writing this book.

Time was up, pencils were down, and papers were collected. Time slowed to a crawl as we waited an eternity for our results. A lady came to read the names of people who had passed. One by one people were rising and leaving the gym. Almost 100 people wrote the test and only 30 would be accepted for the program. When I didn't hear my name, I could feel doubt and disappointment waiting with mouths wide open, ready to swallow me whole. I hung my head as more names were read. Only a few spots left now, my ears fuzzy with failure, I could barely hear the lady reading names. I was jolted out of my hazy trance by a woman jumping up and down, celebrating like a kid next to me. "We made it!" she screamed as she came in for a hug. "We?!" I could barely get myself to pronounce the word. Turns out my name was called, too! I passed the test and was accepted into the course. Relief washed over me. I left school that day knowing I was starting the rest of my life.

I loved school. I loved learning new things, trying something different with my hands, and being creative. I volunteered for a hair show and got my hair done by a famous stylist from California – it was the best cut and colour I've ever had! I also loved my teacher. She was patient and gracious enough to answer all our questions. She owned her own salon and I told her that one day I would, too. I really believed in myself. Since Canada's Wonderland was only a seasonal job, I was out of work while in school, so I became a hairstylist's assistant. It wasn't great money – sometimes they never even paid me, assuming I didn't know the law – but at least it was some money and I was able to gain experience in my field. I worked in this position for a year, gleaning all I could from whoever I was assisting. The owners and stylists were great to help me recognize my strengths and where I needed to learn more. They taught me not only how to cut hair, but people skills as well as how to run your own salon. This experience was priceless compared to all the book knowledge I had acquired.

Eventually, I had enough hours experience to write the exam for my official hairstyling license. It was 200 questions, lasted for 2 hours and cost 100 dollars. I had to get 70% in order to pass. If I failed, a re-take would be completely different questions and cost another 100 dollars. That was money I didn't have, so I had to pass. I purchased the study booklet that went with my exam and was shocked to see that most of the questions pertained to barbers! I didn't study to become a barber, but it's the hand I was dealt. I had to think outside the box if I was going to pass. At that time, I was working in a salon owned by two Italian men who had been in the industry for decades. They were old buddies who loved fashion, hairdressing and had passion for making people look and feel beautiful. Often, they would reminisce with each other over the how the field had changed and grown. From bleached, permed, overly hair sprayed coifs to the sleek layers and highlights of today, these men had seen and tried it all. It was fascinating to hear how they managed to work without the fancy tools and safe products we have now. Some of the techniques and old tools looked like torture devises from medieval times! Thanks to these stories, I was familiar with the older techniques that I found in my study booklet and I was able to pass my exam with 72% on the first try. Dreams really do come true.

Chapter 20

Jenny

That Italian salon I worked at wasn't only good for helping me pass my exam, it's where I met one of my life-long friends, Jenny. We worked at the salon together and would often get together outside of work. We found a place down the street from our salon and on Fridays we'd have dinner together, chat about the week, play pool, drink sour apple martinis, talk about our hopes and dreams, and play more pool. Over time we became very close. Jenny knew I didn't have a lot of money, so she'd often offer to pay the bill. I felt like I was using someone and for the first time in my life, I felt guilty about it – I had come a long way from my time in Israel when my goal was to use anyone as I saw fit. Jenny was always so kind and gracious to me, even on days when I wasn't to her. She never judged me for my behavior, she just loyally stayed by my side. Although Tom had help me along in many ways, I was still a very loud, eccentric girl prone to get mouth after a few drinks were in me. I think that's what I loved so much about Jenny. She was my window into 'normal'; she was serious, calm, well-mannered, and soft spoken – everything I wasn't. Sometimes, I would poke fun at her simple dream of settling down with a man she loved and starting a family. "Why would you want all that nonsense? So much drama, drama, drama..." I would say, "Don't you want to be free and live your life?" I was speaking from heartache, but I didn't know it. With my family background, what did I know of love, of family? I certainly wasn't looking for a serious relationship, let alone love, and yet Jenny accepted me.

Anyway, Jenny was dating the cute bar attender at the bar we'd go to on Friday nights, but the relationship didn't last. They broke up and he moved on very quickly. I could see it was painful for her to witness and it pained me to see her hurting knowing how good she was; she didn't deserve this.

"Tonight is our last night here." I announced on a fateful Friday night. She gave me a knowing look and agreed. We continued playing, drinking, and laughing with the knowledge that it was our last night in our cozy, little bar.

I took a final shot in our game, winning. "I'm the champion!!!" I shouted, not caring who heard me.

"You are so loud, Lena" blushed Jenny.

"Hey, you should be used to it by now" I laughed. But we were interrupted. Someone else across the room was also happily shouting.

Chapter 21

Love at First Sight

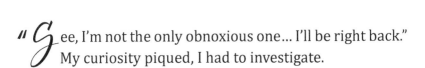

"Gee, I'm not the only obnoxious one... I'll be right back." My curiosity piqued, I had to investigate.

A big guy, 6 feet or so. Black leather jacket, jeans and hair that reminded me of James Dean. He was cheering even though he wasn't playing. I asked him to move pretending he was blocking my way. He turned around and our eyes locked. *What a handsome guy!* I thought to myself. I shuffled past him, pretending not to notice. I went to the balcony for a cigarette and stayed a while. Him and his group of friends came out also, his back turned to me.

"You know, in my country it's rude to turn your back on people. You might get punched in the face for it." I said aggressively. He turned around slowly to see who was mouthing off to him. He was irritated. My tone was not playful. We began to squabble.

"Dude! This girl is hitting on you!'" One of his friends burst in.

"Is it that obvious?" I said through a cheeky grin.

"Not to him." She nodded. I smiled and looked at the boy. He totally understood what was going on and started to laugh. We began talking and carried on until everyone else had left the balcony. Turns out he was at the bar because he had won a poker game and was taking the losers out for drinks. It was his first time at the bar and it was supposed to be my last.

There was something in the way he looked and behaved that attracted me to him like a magnet, a force I couldn't resist. Jenny was not impressed. She wasn't sure if he would be trouble and she knew I was focusing on becoming a hair-stylist. She didn't want to see my dreams derailed over some random guy. But this wasn't a random guy, I could feel it.

We exchanged phone numbers at some point in the early morning when we should have been sleeping. True to his word, he called me the next day and we scheduled a date. Like a gentleman, he took me out, called me beautiful, and made me feel wanted. It wasn't until I noticed that the bartender asked to see his ID when he ordered us drinks that I didn't even know how old this guy was. He looked young, sure, but young enough to be ID'd? I was having second thoughts. In the past, I wouldn't be caught dead with a guy that was even 3 days younger than me... turns out he was six years younger than me. He lived in his grandmother's basement and wore clothes his parents bought for him. I didn't think it would work out, but I got to know him and came to see that he worked hard, was very respectful, had integrity, and carried himself like a mature adult.

My friends would tease me about his age, highlighting the fact that he didn't even own a car. I wasn't looking for love, my friends knew that much, but I was open to someone who was at least rich.

"When your boyfriend gives you a ring you will tell him the diamond is not big enough!" Tom chuckled. He doubted the relationship would last. "If you had a million dollars, would you give him up?" he asked one day, hoping to determine how serious I was. I said not for a million dollars would I leave him and I was serious. Something about this 'baby' boy evoked my heart. Everything with him was new – his manners, his caring nature, his perspective on life. He was young, but there was a deepness to him that I wanted to spend the rest of my days getting to know.

Jenny asked me out for lunch one day. "It's all about him now! I was number one, now this boy is taking up all your time!" She was a little bit upset. I had no defense. Just like Jenny would one day say at our wedding, I fell in love hard and fast.

I have always been strong and independent; I bowed to no one. I made my own rules and did whatever I wanted when I wanted to. I used people and they have used me. Everyone around me served a purpose. Relationships had to benefit me. If I didn't need you –you didn't matter to me. Love wasn't involved into my calculated approach. It was easy to discard people because I wasn't emotionally attached. It was a game. But deep in my heart I knew if I've ever met my match I would be loyal to him for the rest of my life. But I promised myself I would never settle for mediocrity or be forced by my age or simply marry because "everybody does it." I always told myself, that if I were to give my heart away the man would have to be extraordinary – the best of the best. I had high expectations. I craved love, loyalty, respect, kindness, integrity and generosity - everything that my upbringing stole from me.

I knew it was possible; my grandparents were an example of true love. Was it perfect? No, but giving up for them wasn't an option and in the end they were soul mates who left behind a legacy of love. My grandma would often pressure me to choose someone and settle down. I assured her that if I ever found someone good enough, I'd get married and have kids.

Who knew that God was watching me and was planning to fulfill the desires of my heart? Knowing that love would save me, he brought me my husband.

I can't stress enough how surprised I was at his age – he was so young! I couldn't believe that this boy was so young. I used to call him my "baby boy" and "baby G" (for great and grounding, my God). I liked his cheesy jokes, goofing around, and light spirit. But despite his age, this young man was an old soul. He was wise, mature and respectful. He played guitar and brought me flowers, opened the door for me and called me "gorgeous". I felt like a loved woman and I cherished it.

Once day, with a serious tone, he said ... "I don't know what you think about this..." He started so seriously that I teased him... but his next words struck me and all teasing stopped. "I love you and I won't stop pursuing you until you are mine." He was sure 100% that he will succeed. "Love? You're kidding me... Right?" I thought to myself but didn't say anything; something in his tone of voice stopped me from mocking him. But like Jenny had observed, I had already fallen hard. For the first time in my life, I started loving someone other than myself.

"I want to ask you something..." He said after a few dates and I thought, to my surprise, if he asks me to marry him I will say yes! He asked me to move in with him, but I said no. Still, he stuck around and in the time we were together, made me dream of a home, a family and a future- something I have never done before. Nine months later we rented an apartment and moved in together.

In the beginning his family wasn't fond of this situation. We lived together as common law partners and in Ukraine this union was accepted by the government and society. Most of my friends and family had this kind of union, so I couldn't understand why his family wasn't at peace with us. I thought maybe because I'm almost six years older than him or because I have tattoos and my tongue is pierced, or maybe it was the fact that I wasn't 'lady like' or "mother/ wife" material. I wanted a 'normal life' and I found myself committed to making this relationship successful despite all the challenges.

Chapter 22

Pregnant

Two months after we moved in together, I found out I was pregnant. I was overwhelmed with joy and thought to myself that this was exactly what was missing - my own family. But very quickly, panic attacks started swallowing me in fear telling me that it wasn't the right time. I just landed my first real hairstyling job, his family didn't approve of our relationship, I was in the process of getting my permanent residency (wasn't even sure I would be able to stay in Canada!)… the list was a long one.

One day at work, pondering my situation, I began crying. My friend and co-worker reached out and asked me, " Well … what do YOU want?" Such a simple and profound question. "I love this man and I want to have his baby." I said 100% sure. I didn't know what to expect when I told him I wanted to keep the baby. His reaction was priceless. He wanted to be a father. He brought me flowers and took care of me like a queen. Of course, like all new parents we had moments when the fear of the unknown was overpowering but we got through it together.

I loved this man and this beautiful tiny baby in my belly with all my heart. I announced the news to my grandma knowing she would approve, but we dreaded telling his parents. They were traditional people, still unapproving of us living together – what would they say now that a baby was on the way? But, keeping it a secret wasn't an option – a baby isn't something you can hide. We figured they'd be more hurt the longer we waited.

"Baba" -his Ukrainian grandma- was so clever. She knew. At a family gathering one time, she happily exclaimed that I was expecting and gently touched my growing belly. She spoke Ukrainian, but no one paid attention because they didn't understand the language. "I am just fat, baba, I quit exercising." I laughed her off in a panic. At dinner I was able to eat my food and leftovers. I am not sure how they didn't think it was suspicious or weird. I guess I always did have an appetite…

We made the decision to announce my pregnancy to his family. We invited them over and they sat on our big L-shaped couch, creating an audience of critics. It was nerve wracking. I didn't want to burn the bridge between him and his family. They are very close. His sister-in-law came across our ultrasound pictures that we had lying on our shelf and excitedly asked if we were expecting. Embarrassed that we left those out for someone to discover, I was about to answer her from the kitchen when I heard him blurt out loud and clear:

"We are having a baby!!!" I almost dropped the salad I was preparing. My hands were shaking, my throat was dry and I felt like I was going to pass out. I came out and saw faces frozen with fear and confusion. I stood beside my man waiting for the verdict. But he continued, "If you want to be a part of our life you are welcome to stay. If not you can leave. She is my family now." I heard the seriousness in his voice. I knew he wasn't kidding. In that moment I fell in love with him even more. I knew I belonged with this man. He had my back, he was my rock.

His family were shocked and there were some tears, for sure, but no one left. They loved him and were willing to love me too. His mom called me the next day and we talked for 2 hours. I was glad that she was trying to know me. "This is not how we do things, but my son loves you, and the Lord has a plan for you... We will trust in Him." She was wise, kind and soft-spoken as she slowly began to embrace me into her family.

With that trial behind me, I began imagining my future as a parent. I loved my belly and all the movements of growing life inside me. But this was not an easy time for me. Ksenia's little face would appear in my mind as well as the abortions I had had – I doubted my competency as a mother. Always worried that I would turn out like my mother, I had lots of fear to work through. Slowly I was transitioning into becoming a stay-at-home mom and a housekeeper, which was foreign to me. Some women dream about it whole their lives. Not me, I was petrified. I wasn't a "natural" at any of it, but I knew I wanted to do my best! I decided I would fake it until I had learned how to deal with this new situation - motherhood. I told myself that I would adjust, adapt, and succeed like I always had. I was resilient. Despite my 'fake it till you make it' plan, I could not make it work. The routine of chores, the loneliness of being home, and the hormone imbalance from being pregnant hit me like a truck.

My rebellious selfish nature didn't want to submit and surrender to my new condition. Fear and frustration began to overwhelm me. I was failing. I quickly lost everything I drew my worth and value from. My figure, my looks, my strength-emotional and physical- my job, my sports and my freedom. I lost my identity. I wasn't who I was before but not yet who I wanted to be. I didn't like me. I got depressed. I felt trapped.

Chapter 23

It's a ... boy? girl?

$\mathcal{S}$ ince the very beginning I wanted to know sex of the baby. I like to be prepared and ready. I love to plan and hate when something goes wrong. So, we decided to find out. "It's a boy." I got the answerer to my curiosity and I felt... disappointed. I felt bad for being disappointed, but couldn't help it. I always thought I would have a girl. For many generations in my family we had females. We are strong independent leaders with powerful stories.

"Be grateful that you are having a baby, as long as he is healthy blah, blah, blah." I kept saying to myself trying to convince my mind and heart and obtain peace. It didn't make any difference in the way I felt about it.

My boyfriend, on the other hand, was so excited. He was going to be a father! We had chosen a name for our son. We bought a khaki color stroller and painted nursery green. We bought clothes, toys, and books. I was ready for my son's arrival. I started to feel comfortable and relaxed, everything was going as planned.

I loved being pregnant this time around, especially since it was a fairly easy one – not too much discomfort. In fact, I found that my senses – my taste buds and smelling especially – were awakened. Everything tasted and smelled especially delicious. My body, even though it was changing, was beautiful. I came to love my belly. Especially feeling my baby moving inside. It's an extraordinary and marvelous sensation to feel life growing inside of you.

One night I had a dream. I was sitting on the edge of a fountain in the middle of a mall. I was pregnant and in front of me I saw a beautiful little girl. She was about 4 years old. I looked at her with delight and felt my love for her. Concerned for my well-being she gently patted my tummy and asked if I was ok. In that instant I knew–this is my child! My daughter! I woke up trying to find an explanation for this dream. As you know, dreams have often played a significant role in my life. I was confused, worried, and cautiously optimistic with this little glimpse of hope.

"What does it mean? Is it the past? Future? Or just fantasy? Could it be true?" I began asking myself. I reminded myself that I was having a boy, concluded it was just a dream and chose not to pursue this useless trail of hope.

At the beginning of my third trimester I received a phone call. I was having some complications and had to get an emergency ultrasound done to determine if I would need a c-section to deliver. The ultrasound was finished and I was about to get up when the sonographer asked me:

"Would you like to know sex of the baby?"

"Nah, it's a boy." I brushed him off coldly.

"Who told you that?" I froze in disbelief and confusion. Little spark of hope ... could it be true? I felt like time stopped

I kept starring bluntly at the monitor with the blurry black and white picture.

"Do you speak English? Can you read?" He pulled me out of my trance.

"Yes..." I said slowly.

He pointed his cursor on the screen with my baby's picture and typed: I AM A GIRL! My jaw dropped, my heart was pounding so hard I thought I would faint. I couldn't believe it. My dream came true. It was a secret desire of my heart and I never told anyone that I wanted a daughter. It was a miracle. I called my boyfriend and told him we were having a daughter... he hung up on me, needing a minute to digest. He called me back and said:

"It's a baby and I'm grateful. As long as she is healthy..."

Shortly after this, my friend called. "You are going to think I'm crazy, but I had a dream. YOU ARE GOING TO HAVE A BABY GIRL! Start throwing out your boy stuff! I will bring you girls' clothes. My daughters stuff." I was shocked that my dreams were coming true.

"You are right -it's a girl. I found out this morning." I said slowly remembering my dream.

So, all of a sudden, I was not ready at all. My perfectly crafted plan crumbled...but I was overjoyed. God's plan is always better! I kept saying thank you over and over again. I wasn't a Christian then and didn't even know who I was thanking.

Chapter 24

Our Firstborn

I got the news that our baby was going to be a girl on a Friday and on the following Tuesday she was born... 5 weeks early! I didn't realize I was in labor and for a couple days suffered through severe back pain, thinking it was just normal aches and pains. I had an appointment with a lady from the bank who was helping us starting a saving's bond that we decided to have for the baby. She was so energetic and talkative. I liked her, but not today. I called my midwife and she recommended going to the hospital.

"It could be an infection or early labor, ether way we have to make sure that baby is ok. Bring your husband as well."

My boyfriend rushed home. We didn't own a car so "bond" lady volunteered to drive us to the hospital. She giggled and chatted all the way while I was dying on the back seat. Our midwife met us there. Tests determined that I didn't have an infection, but that our baby was very active. We waited for the doctor on call.

"You will have a baby tonight!" Announced the doctor after conducting an internal examination.

"Wait. What? NO! I'm not ready!" I panicked. For all my planning and prepping, I ended up in the hospital with only my purse and pair of socks. My boyfriend was so excited, "I've got to call my mom!" he said.

"Don't you dare leave me here alone!" I was threating him. I was so scared.

In the hospital I wanted an epidural...I didn't care. I needed drugs. My boyfriend was trying to help me by reminding how we learned to breath at prenatal classes... Wasn't a good idea! I grabbed him and my nails went deep into his skin. The nurse couldn't find my veins to start IV. No IV - no epidural. Doctor was unavailable. He was performing an emergency C-section. My midwife was gone to have a break. My poor boyfriend was doing all he could to make me more comfortable. It wasn't easy for him to see me suffering. I felt a pop inside of me, almost like a champagne bottle was opened, and my pain multiplied. I screamed:

"My water broke!!!" I felt muscles were stretching and tearing. Her body was pushing through mine.

"Don't push doctor is not here yet." Frantically said the nurse.

"Don't push???" I screamed. "Baby is coming!" I felt her moving through my body with a tight painful force. My body itself was pushing her out. My boyfriend called my midwife. When she came, he said with confidence:

"Tell me what to do." I think at some point I lost consciousness because I can't recall anything. He said I was screaming, arching my back and rolling my eyes so far back it was all white. He said it was like a horror movie. The doctor rushed in to deliver the baby. He was very busy that night. He cut the umbilical cord, which was wrapped around baby's neck and got her out safely. They took her into incubator on another floor.

In the rush of the moment, the doctor didn't check if my placenta delivered intact. It wasn't and I was bleeding internally – I lost a lot of blood that night. My boyfriend was panicking as he saw me passing in out of consciousness. My heart was pounding and ringing in my ears, making me deaf, except for the sound of my thoughts telling me I was going to die. My body trembled with fear and weakness. I kept falling into the darkness of unconsciousness, as if life was pulling the plug and disconnecting me from my physical existence. With each black out, I could feel death closer. I was worried that the next time would be the last time. I panicked and screamed my boyfriend's name while frantically trying to grab onto something familiar that would keep me on this side of reality.

I smelled blood and I could taste it in my mouth. I asked him to lie down beside me so I could smell his cologne. It gave me comfort camouflaging the metallic smell and taste of my own blood. The nurse kept changing my bloody sheets. No one called the doctor...

"How could they think this was normal?" I couldn't understand why no one checked on me.

There was a shift change and new doctor came to do his rounds. He was shocked to find me still bleeding and that no one had taken the responsibility to figure out why. He cleaned out my uterus by scrubbing out the leftover placenta pieces out of me while four other people held me down. His hand was in me almost up to his elbow as he scrubbed walls of my uterus like I scrub seeds from inside of the butternut squash with the spoon. It was more painful than the delivery itself. I screamed and ripped the skin from my boyfriend's arms with my nails.

I lost so much blood that I needed to get a blood transfusion, but no one could find my veins. They collapsed in stressful situations. A few doctors, including their best anesthesiologist, tried with no luck. "If you would lose 52% (I've lost 50%) of your blood, we would treat it as an emergency and cut artery in your inner thigh and put the tubes in. But you are young and healthy so you will recover". He concluded! If I could have stood up I would have punched him in the face. Their negligence caused this and still they didn't fix it.

I didn't see my daughter for 3 days. My boyfriend took care of me: he fed me, ran around getting nurses, trying his best to keep calm. He was sleeping beside me on the folding chair. He was tired physically and emotionally. I was so busy with myself I didn't even realize how much of a toll it took on him. To think he might lose the baby and mother in the same night. By the grace of God, we both survived and the long road to recovery began.

Our daughter was in the nursery on the same floor. My boyfriend was able to visit her. He was talking to the doctors and her nurses bringing me updates and pictures. She was a good size for a premature baby - 5.7 lbs. She had a good body temperature and even had sucking reflexes, which is unusual in these cases.

My nurse was a tall (almost 6 ft.) Russian lady. She said, "It's ok if baby small. She will survive. Trust me I know. I was preemie as well, not even 3 pounds. After delivery, my mom put me in a shoebox beside her bed. Then she nursed me. And look at me now" she added with a chuckle. "Babies not as fragile as you might think".

Her stories encouraged me. At least my baby was in the hospital under the care of professionals.

She was in an incubator for the first day and then they decided that she would be fine without it. Her father was so proud of her. He was tearing up telling me her progress and showing me her pictures and videos. She looked like little alien. Pink, wrinkly, with closed, shiny, eyelids.

He was completely comfortable with his new role as a father. He was a natural. In this moment I loved him even more. For the first time (through this difficult situation) I saw my boyfriend put his trust in God. I knew his heart belonged to Jesus. He prayed, crying out to God giving thanks for small and significant improvements. He cared for me with love and compassion, slowly nursing me back to life. I gave my heart to him and he proved to be the right man for me.

The nurse brought me forms to fill out - baby's birth certificate and other official documents. I realized then that we hadn't chosen a name for her. We brainstormed ideas. I loved a name from a movie I saw, there was a queen warrior, beautiful, powerful and smart and the name means to rival or excel. Her father liked a name which meant bright, clear. And that's who she is, powerful, bright force!

I wanted to hold my baby so bad. My boyfriend took me there on a wheel chair and I couldn't contain my excitement. She was tiny and beautiful, my daughter. She had a blanket and little pink knitted hat no bigger than my fist, generously donated by volunteers. I held her fascinated by this tiny human being. Powerful emotions of love and gratitude, that I have healthy daughter, swelled up inside of me. I was overwhelmed with joy. This time I would be leaving the hospital with my own little bundle of joy.

Chapter 25

Changing Dynamics

*I*n a week I was discharged from the hospital, but without the baby. My daughter had to stay for a few more days under medical observation. I felt awful – memories of Ksenia and leaving the hospital empty handed kept popping up. I abandoned my daughter – again. Fear that I was turning out just like my mother drove me to risk my life and take the bus to get to the hospital. I know I needed to recover, but I was torn with the need to be there for my baby girl.

On these journeys to the hospital, I was alone, helpless and scared. My boyfriend had to return to work almost immediately – he has a very demanding job. When he found out that I was going to the hospital on my own to be with my daughter, he was angry and afraid for me. I had a need that he couldn't understand. I *needed* to be close to my baby. I vowed that this time would be different – I couldn't leave my baby girl, I *wouldn't*.

Finally, she was cleared to go home and our journey as parents began! Having a newborn at home was stressful and exhausting. We didn't know what we were doing (I wonder if any parent does...)! We started fighting almost daily – hungry and tired, we had no energy to get along or be civil. Among the many stressful moments, one stands out in my memory – the first time she got sick. Her little nose was so full of mucous that she couldn't breathe. She turned blue. We both panicked and called 911. Her father vigorously patted her back in fear. He shook her upside down until she cried. I froze paralyzed with fear. I never loved and cared for any human being as much as I cared for this child. The pang of hopelessness pierced my heart – my daughter was going to die. Tears were flowing down my face as I held my baby girl. An ambulance was downstairs in minutes and they took us to the hospital. The doctor decided to keep us overnight for observation. I was grateful for the medical professionals, but their expertise did nothing to calm my ever-growing anxiety around protecting my baby girl. Nothing could give me solace.

Looking back, it's hard to picture her as the fragile baby that she was, so delicate requiring such tender care. Having had no example of tender motherhood myself, her father took it upon himself to take care of those things while I caught up to the idea of being a mother to such a fragile human – bathing her, cutting her nails, etc. She grew up fast... cute and perfectly chubby. *My daughter* - beautiful, emotional, bright, passionate and amazing. She was and is my biggest challenge; my crash course on parenting. Be careful what you wish for: dreaming to have a daughter the same as myself backfired. She is exactly like me! Stubborn and passionate. As if to foreshadow her life of independence, she started walking at 13 months which was too early for me! Fall after fall, she was determined to lift herself up over and over again. She did a few steps at home, then a few days later at a family gathering she ran across the living room with 11 steps in count! Our baby was walking and hasn't stopped since.

Apart from the daily tasks of taking care of a baby's needs, I realized that I was also tasked with raising this little girl to be a woman – the most daunting element of parenthood, for sure. Although I was in a secure relationship with a loving partner, it didn't erase my history of abuse and neglect. Feelings of inadequacy often took over and I felt out of control. I had no real example of parenting to fall back on besides the memory of my grandma's discipline. Remembering this, I tried to be strong and controlling. One day I was looking into my daughter's eyes and she was staring right back, eyes flickering with defiance. "You are 3 and I'm 30! How dare you!" I thought to myself. I was losing it. I was astonished that I couldn't control a 3-year-old kid! But I didn't give up. I turned to my boyfriend and disclosed my feelings of inadequacy and how lost I felt. He met me there, comforted me, and reminded me that we were in this together. We had to learn from each other, changing, adopting, and creating new strategies for raising this strong-willed child. If not for her sake, for the sake of our relationship! A new baby can put strain on a relationship in ways we hadn't anticipated. Even now, we are still learning – always making mistakes, but always learning from them. We make a good team.

Even though I knew I wasn't alone – I had my boyfriend – fear and anxiety still permeated my life. Whenever my baby would get sick, I would crumble. A voice would say to me, "Your daughter is going to die! Look at her - you can't do anything! You are a failure and a useless mother. Then your precious boyfriend will blame you for it and leave you. You will end up on the streets again". In this anxious lifestyle, I must have brought her to emergency room 100 times before she hit 3 years old. Most of the time I heard every-thing was normal – kids get sick! One particular instance, my boyfriend turned to me and said "Why are you stressed? You are a good mother. This child does not belong to you. Her life belongs to God. He is responsible for her. So it's not up to you what happens to her. He gave us our daughter to care and raise and guide. We have to do what we can, but the outcome is up to Him."

I started to believe in some way there was a God who cared for me, though I didn't really know what that meant. His words and beliefs set me free, though it would be a while until his beliefs became my beliefs. It took the responsibility for her life from my shoulders. He told me he would never blame me. This revelation gave me new perspective. I knew she was a gift to me because I don't deserve to be a mother. God choose me to have her. He watches over her. It gave me peace that God is in control. (...Do not be anxious about anything, but in every situation, by prayer and petition, with thanksgiving, present your request to God. And the peace of God, which transcends all understanding, will guard your hearts and your minds in Christ Jesus. Philippians 4:6-7 NIV) Prayer doesn't have to be a perfect poem...I had this weapon whenever I felt panic and fear crippling my mind, I would shout out loud: "God take care of my baby! Please, take care of my baby!" It helped me switch my attention from fear to God. My circumstances were the same, but my focus switched enabling me to deal with situation on hand.

Chapter 26

Jesus

It was in this rocky first few years of parenthood, that I really got a glimpse of my boyfriend's faith-based upbringing and the foundation on which he lived his life. He was born and raised in a Christian home, son of a pastor (funny how I catapulted from halfway around the world and landed right in the middle of a Christ-loving family – not a coincidence!). The fourth child of a large, protective family. As I've said, they didn't approve of our living arrangement - tolerated it but weren't excited about it. Sometimes, I heard from them, "You are living in sin because you are not married..." It was more like a statement of fact rather than condemnation. To me, it was some kind of religious Christian cliché - it didn't mean a thing to me, like they were speaking a language I didn't know. But still, they accepted us and never told us what to do – never told us to get married, never told us how to raise my daughter, didn't make us go to church, didn't force me to quit smoking. I was glad they gave us space to be who we were – I would not have taken well to being told what to do! His mother always just quietly said, "I'm praying for you ..." and she was genuine. This family wasn't perfect, but they were *different*. They had a love and respect for Jesus Christ and his Word. It wasn't like any dry religion that I had encountered throughout my life time – they seemed to have a real relationship with Christ. It reminded me of my Christian friends in Ukraine who helped me get clean. Like them, this family was genuinely seeking something and were visibly different as a result.

I never experienced anything like this. I saw this in my boyfriend when I met him – virtues absent in everyone else I had come across in life. He was patient, kind, and just *good.* He was faithful, loving, and full of integrity. I was always amazed that someone so young could possess all those qualities. I started worshiping him because I felt loved and protected and cared for...I didn't know then that I worshiped the Fruit of the Spirit that was within this man. Being in a relationship with him prepared my heart to fall in love with Jesus and to put Him on the throne of my heart. Until then, my boyfriend was my everything.

His family often invited us to Christmas and Easter services, and we went to church with them to be polite. I couldn't understand what the pastor was saying but I loved the atmosphere – nice music and beautiful singing. I often got the sense that at church I could be someone else - like there was some refresh button I could press that could give me a chance at a new life. Not that I was willing to 'press that button' just yet, but for a moment I could dream of being someone different.

It wasn't new and exciting for my boyfriend. He came to be with his family. He was practically raised in the church and frankly got fed up with it. Faith is a matter of free will and he felt like he never had a choice. He wanted the freedom to choose, so he did! Only he chose the opposite direction and that's when we met. I was the complete opposite of all the Christian girls he had known and that's part of what attracted him to me. In the same way, he was unlike anyone I had ever met but because he was *so good*. No matter how bad he thought he was, I knew he was an angel compared to me.

As you know, when I arrived to Canada my English was not so good and needed a lot of work. I'm still surprised that he was able to understand me, my accent was still so thick when we met! Even now, it's not perfect and even my daughter has to spell words for me. My understanding was good, but if people had accents – British or Indian – it was very difficult for me. This might be why I never really paid any attention to what the pastor was saying at church. He was from India, spoke very fast, and was very educated. He used a lot of big words and phrases and I could never quite capture the full meaning of what he was talking about, so my mind would wander. But I would always be intrigued by the intensity of his emotion. There were times when he'd be passionately making a point, fighting back tears. Men don't cry where I come from, so whatever he was talking about had to be serious, something very important, I thought. But I started to wonder *why* – why care so much about this abstract idea of God?

Whenever we would go to church, I wanted to sit all the way in the back on the balcony. Any time we sat near the front, something would happen inside me. I don't know how to describe it other than I would just 'feel' something and often cry... a lot! So much so, people I didn't even know would approach me, trying to console me, offering to pray for me. One woman told me it was the Holy Spirit washing out my soul. I thought that was just weird and embarrassing, so we hid in the balcony. It felt nice and safe ... far from anything 'weird'.

But even there, where I thought I was protecting myself from anything too crazy, my life changed. For the first time, I really heard and understood the Gospel message – that Christ came to this earth as God, died for our sins, and rose again, breaking the bondage of sin and restoring us to himself. My mind and heart were opened. That day I knew God was calling me! It was impossible, extraordinary and exciting all at the same time. I wanted to come to church more often to hear this pastor speak – suddenly his accent wasn't a hindrance. I loved to hear his sermons, now they all made sense. My eyes and my ears were open. My heart was yearning for more. This man loved Jesus with all his mind, soul and strength – an amazing example of a dedicated follower of Christ – and the complete opposite of me. He was born in India, got his degree at MIT in Boston, and then came to Canada to work in the field of atomic energy, spending 11 years as a safety analyst for nuclear powerplants. He was very active with Youth for Christ in India and in Boston with Campus for Christ. When he came to Toronto, his primary ministry was as an adult Christian Education teacher at his church. He moved on to serve as a member of the Executive Committee at this same church where eventually he would become the senior pastor. He also holds an honorary doctorate from the Canadian Bible College and Theological Seminary in Regina, Canada. Why am I telling you all this information about my pastor? Because this is whom God chose to lead me to Him. On the one hand, here is a highly educated, intelligent Pastor, who has so much love and passion for Christ and His Word on the other was me – a Ukrainian immigrant, with broken English, a murky past, and limited knowledge of God and the Bible. One day he said, "I hope and pray you will see me as a bridge between you and Christ ... don't admire my talents and my abilities because it has been given to me by God to serve Him for His Glory." It hit me – this man wasn't living for himself, he was living for God and through this example – this bridge - I came to know God for myself.

Even though we started coming to church more regularly, there was a lot I still didn't understand. One day after church, my mother-in-law approached me and said, "I signed you guys up for a course at our church. You need to spend some time together. You will have a nice dinner and watch a video, then discuss it. Plus, you can make new friends. I will babysit for you". The course was Alpha and it covered a bunch of topics about Christianity: Who is Jesus? Why read the Bible? How does God guide us? What is the church? This was exactly what I was looking for – a place to explore and learn more about my new faith in a non-invasive overly religious way! It was there that I prayed the prayer of salvation and gave my life to Christ.

... Everyone who calls on the name of the Lord will be saved.
Acts 2:21 (NLT)

It was there that I was 'saved'. It felt like a weight was lifted from my shoulders. Now the Lord is the Spirit, and where the Spirit of the Lord is, there is freedom. 2 Corinthians 3:17. I chose to believe Christ is my Lord and my Savior. He died for me! For me... He was the missing piece that filled the void inside my heart. He will never leave me and never forsake me and He will never give up on me.

Chapter 27

Pearls

I had a vision where God was hovering over the "dump." He was looking for something with excitement. Something shiny caught His attention. Something really hard to see it was so dirty, but He knew... the potential was endless. He stops and picks that piece up. He smiles. Cleans it by breathing on it, then shines it on his robes. It's a beautiful pearl! He goes home, shows it to His Dad, holding the pearl carefully and tenderly in the palm of His hand. He is delighted. His treasure. His gem. From now on He will care for and protect it. He puts this pearl with other precious jewels, and He says: "Here is your home now. Here you belong. Here you will shine. Here you will bring joy to others and here I will care for you. You are significant, priceless, and precious to me."

That pearl is ME! I believe I am God's treasure. I was lost and now I'm found...I gave my life to Christ because He first loved me. If you think I am special- you are correct. I am a sinner whose Father is God! If God didn't ask me to reveal my story I would bury my past under a rock so nobody could ever find it. I didn't run to volunteer to show all my dirt before meeting Jesus. I have a reputation to protect and a certain carefully crafted image of how I wanted people to perceive me; a Christian wife with 3 beautiful children passionate about serving! I didn't want them to know about the little, broken girl from Ukraine.

I love when people ask me if I was born into Christian family. They see Christ in me! But I know the truth can encourage and help someone to see that God doesn't make exceptions. He doesn't care about your place of birth, your circumstances, or your past. His Salvation is a FREE GIFT for EVERYONE.

"But to all who did receive Him, who believed in His name, He gave the right to become children of God." John1: 12 ESV. For by grace you have been saved through faith. And this is not your own doing; it is the gift of God, not a result of your works, so that no one may boast."
Ephesians 2:8-9 ESV

Throughout my life kindness and compassion shone through me unexpectedly. I always thought these traits were my biggest weaknesses, but God revealed to me that they are actually my strengths. My true nature is to love and be loved. God showed me miracles that were both unexplainable and extraordinary. He blessed me beyond all measure. He is the God Who hears my prayers and feels my pain. In the past I called these perfectly timed miracles 'positive energy' or 'good luck', but I was wrong. I always knew that everything happens for a reason.

I want to show in this book that God is REAL! God healed me, restored me, redeemed me, blessed me, loved me, strengthened me, and gave me His peace, forgiveness and mercy. HE LOVED ME FIRST before I even knew anything about Him! The best decision I ever made was to follow Him. If you are considering this or are interested, I encourage you to reach out to someone at a church. Don't let the opportunity pass you by. If a little voice is nudging you, listen.

Chapter 28

Becoming a Follower

I had spent my whole life as a leader – my life, my way. Meeting the love of my life forced me to compromise in some ways, but I still had a stubborn edge. Meeting Jesus, however, changed everything. I realized that becoming a Christian meant become a Christ *follower*. There were things about my life that needed to change so that I could become more like Him.

For years, my boyfriend had struggled to find the right title for me. We had been living together for four years now and he still didn't know what to call me. "I'm not your girlfriend or partner! I have your child! I'm cleaning and cooking for you! I am your *wife*!" I was frustrated.

"But you are not my wife... we are not married" Was his reply.

It made me angry and I was hurt. I never thought that you had to be 'married' to be husband and wife. Back home, common law unions were called "civil marriages" and the couple was legally husband and wife. I couldn't understand what his problem was until I met Jesus. I realized then that a wedding is so much more than a ceremony. The Holy Spirit confronted us both about living in sin. It became awkward to be intimate. Being together felt wrong! It was weird, but we didn't talk about it. We avoided the difficult conversation because we didn't know that both of us felt the same. When I finally spit it out my boyfriend told me he felt the same. We both felt like strangers living under one roof.

Our 5th year anniversary was coming up and we had planned a nice date to celebrate the occasion. We dropped our daughter off at grandma's and went to a beautiful restaurant. We ordered delicious food and some wine. After a glass, I was feeling a little lighted headed – I hadn't drank in a while. While we were waiting for dessert, he steered the conversation to a more serious note. He began saying how thankful he was for me and how much he loved me.

"Lena, you are a good mother. I love you so much and can't imagine my life without you..." I thought to myself that if he carried on being so sweet like this, we wouldn't even need dessert! But, feeling the wine a little, I didn't pick up on any cues that he might be preparing for something. I knew he loved me, but this show was not like him. While I was trying to figure out what he was up to, I realized that I hadn't been paying attention to what he was actually saying. Next thing I knew, he was kneeling, and I was staring at a diamond ring! I'm still not even sure if he had even asked me anything, but I was shouting, "YES! YES! YES!" It finally hit me - he was proposing! I had wanted nothing more than to become this man's wife and it was finally happening! In the bathroom, looking at the ring, I squealed with excitement ready for the next steps. A profound sense of gratitude also washed over me – never in my life did I think a man like him would propose to a woman like me – I was thankful that God had orchestrated all of this.

I know some people say that marriage doesn't mean anything, that it's just a piece of paper and I used to be one of those people! But the first time he referred to me as his wife, I cried. I was so proud of my new title and everything that came along with it. We had a beautiful ceremony, where Tom walked me down the aisle. Even though we had been together for 5 years, our marriage felt like the beginning of something – our life together with Christ.

Later that year I decided to be baptized so I could publicly declare God as my Lord and my Savior. I was "on fire" for Christ and was excited to take this step of obedience. As part of the process, I was asked to share a bit of my testimony and it gave me a good opportunity to reflect on where God had brought me from and what he brought me to. As I was reflecting though, I felt a fear well up inside me as I thought about the beautiful life I now had. Becoming a follower was about obedience, but I was worried about everything God would ask me to do. I was thinking about the story from the bible about Abraham and Isaac and how God asked Abraham to sacrifice his own son out of obedience. This story confused me as I contemplated taking my own step of obedience, baptism. I was afraid God would ask me to sacrifice my own child! In that moment, I decided since I could never sacrifice my own child perhaps, I shouldn't get baptized.

Thankfully, I have people in my life that I can share my thoughts with – the good and the crazy. I shared these fears with my mother-in-law – how I was worried that God would require me to do things I wouldn't want to do. She reminded me that fear and confusion do not come from God and encouraged me to challenge these thoughts. "Imagine you are a knight, protected in armor" she said and pointed me to the scripture about the armour of God in Ephesians 6:10-18. I love old movies and have a strong imagination, so this was not hard for me to do. I got back to working on my testimony and the same fears crept up, but this time I knew I was covered by the grace of God in his armor. "He loves me!" I said, as I challenged the fears. I pictured myself on a battlefield with a sword raised. My sword started to shine, like the rays of the sun. I did not go to battle alone, God was with me, so I began writing bits of my story.

I wrote about how I came from an atheist family and never knew God, but that he found me and saved me. I left out the finer details – I wasn't ready to share *that* much – but focused on how God had brought me from so far and was transforming me to look more like Him. On the day of my baptism I felt terrified to speak in front of the church but standing in that pool and looking out at the audience, all I saw was bright lights and the darkness beyond. It was surreal. I knew everyone was there, but it felt like I was talking to God Himself. Then I heard my husband's voice. He blessed me with words of encouragement. He used his father's favorite scripture. "For God gave us a Spirit not of fear but of Power and Love and Self-Control" 2 Timothy 1:7. It was beautiful.

In the process leading up to baptism, I had to attend some classes so I could be sure I understood what I was doing. The pastor leading the class asked us if we really believed we'd go to heaven now that we had accepted Christ. At that moment all my life, all my mistakes, rebellion and wickedness rushed through my mind. "No" I said firmly. He would never let me into heaven; I am not worthy and don't deserve it. I was only hoping for a better life here on earth. The pastor corrected me, "You will go to heaven! Jesus washed away your sin with his blood. It's not your works, but his love that saves you!". My eyes filled with tears. Not only did I get a second chance, but I was starting over with a clean slate – nothing would be held against me. It says in scripture, "His love for His followers is as high as heaven is above the earth. And He has taken our sins as far away from us as the east is from the west." (Psalm 103:11-12 ERV.) One of my favorite preachers, Joyce Meyer, refers to this as "special grace for a special case." This love, grace and mercy made me fall in love with Jesus even more. When I came out of the water that day, I chose to believe that my old sin was dead and that I was a new creation.

Chapter 29

Sharing Christ

Raising my own kids I can often be tough on my own parents. Painful memories resurface as I remember how they failed to be there for me time and time again. Feelings of anger, bitterness and resentment often bubble to the surface and it can be difficult to remember anything good. Being the oldest child, there was a brief moment where I did have a taste of a "normal" family life. But as you know, my parents focused on themselves and what made them happy dissolving any chance of a normal, loving family for me. When I left home, I didn't keep in touch with them very often. The last time I had spent time with my father was when I lived with him in the country before moving to Israel. My mother? I'm not sure when I ever spent time with her, to be honest. We had no relationship. Anger and resentment rooted deeply in my heart. I became cold and mean towards them because I was broken, abandoned and miserable. *Mean people are hurting inside. That's why they act like that. They need love, mercy, and special grace* is what I tell my kids when they're mistreated. I know this because I was that broken person, lashing out at everyone around me.

Before becoming a Christian, I didn't know what to do with all this anger and resentment. It was a part of me for so long and helped form so much of my identity that I wasn't sure what to do with it. It protected me and was the fuel I needed in order to survive in all the ways I've shared with you. After coming to know Christ, I realized I had to forgive them... not because of anything they did to warrant forgiveness, but because Jesus forgave me. I realized that the anger and resentment I was harboring wasn't protecting me, it was stealing my joy. I tried to accomplish this on my own. I decided that enough was enough. Whenever I would remember them, I forced myself to think about the glimmers of good things they did. Repeating these things over and over, I thought I could change the way I thought about them. "Hate the sin not the person" became my motto. I told myself that without my parents I wouldn't be born, that they made me who I was, that all the struggles brought me to where I was now. I tried all the positive thinking, but nothing was changing. My anger and hurt still pulsed within me.

At the same time, I knew God was dealing with the wrongdoings in my past. As I continually came to terms with the things I had done, but that Christ was washing those deeds away, I slowly realized that I could do the same for my parents. During this spiritual journey, my feelings eventually caught up with my thoughts. I was finally able to forgive my parents and let go of the pain and hurt they caused me. Again, my parents didn't change, nor did my childhood, but I had a different perspective now. I was able to love my parents with all their flaws, like God loved me. This was perhaps one of the biggest ways in which God grew my faith in him. I trusted him with this pain and forgave my parents.

I knew I had forgiven my parents the day I realized I was ready to start building a relationship with them again. I hadn't talked to my father in 12 years. He was in Ukraine living in a remote village all alone with no phone or Internet. When he got sick, miraculously we reconnected. He bought a cell phone and we were able to talk almost every day, slowly building a relationship we never had. Eventually, I told him that I forgave him for everything and that I loved him.

When I said this to him, he cried. I could hear the guilt and condemnation thick in his voice as he said that he could never understand how I was able to forgive him. "It's all about God, dad" and I told him about my relationship with Jesus. I told him how Christ had set me free from my sin and how I was a new creation. I talked about how God had forgiven me and how I gave Him all my hurt and pain in return for peace and joy. I never thought that I would ever have a conversation like this with my father. He didn't like to hear anything concerning God or faith or prayer at all. But when his own daughter was speaking of these things, this was evidence he could not refuse- my life was transformed! The difference, before and after, was so significant that he couldn't help but be curious. Who is this Jesus who saves and restores and drastically changes lives?

My father's health rapidly declined, and maybe that was the reason for his seeking. He had a lump on his neck that grew bigger, becoming more painful. Doctors gave him painkillers but couldn't figure out what was causing this issue. Finally, they sent my dad to the city nearby and did numerous tests where they confirmed that my dad had throat cancer. The medications that he was on at the time weakened his heart and because of it no doctor wanted to operate on him. "I don't want your death on my operating table to be a black mark on my perfect record." One doctor said to him bluntly.

At this news, my dad became depressed and angry. Doctors gave him 6 months to live. It was scary and very sad. I felt like I just got him back into my life and was losing him again. I now felt the urgency to share the Gospel even more. I told him about God and His miracles in my life. I told him that it was only by the grace of God that I've been saved to be a faithful wife and loving mother.

"God is powerful, and I trust in Him and His plan. I know you are terrified, and I will be praying for you." I was crying when I told him this. He awkwardly chuckled and said, "I'm not young anymore, I've lived my life..." trying to appear brave, but I caught the pain and regret in his voice. He didn't object to my "religious talk" and it encouraged my boldness. I know he was starting to feel the tiny possibility that he could be forgiven too, a small glimmer of hope. I believe that ultimately all of us want to go to heaven. No one in their right mind will say, "I would love to spend my eternity in hell!" Everyone knows hell is not the place you want to end up in. Especially not for eternity.

One day after church, I asked my friends to pray for my dad and my family back home. I was surprised when they knelt right down on the sanctuary floor holding hands together and inviting me to do the same. That's what's different about "church" people - they will be there for you. I joined them. Staying on our knees we prayed out loud taking turns asking God to intervene. We prayed for peace and comfort, protection from fear and unity for my family in these difficult times. I wanted for my dad to know Jesus and His love, so we also prayed for his salvation. The words flowed easily, sounding eloquent – the Holy Spirit was at work. I felt loved and comforted by God knowing that He was orchestrating this moment. He loved my family through His disciples who were praying with me.

While we prayed, I had a vision. I was hugging my dad and holding him very tight. I felt his body tremble with pain and fear of death. The grace and peace of God entered his body through me and he became relaxed and calm in my embrace. At that moment I experienced God's powerful and beautiful presence. My body was shaking, my heart was racing while the "peace of God, which transcends all under-standing…" filled my body. It was such an unusual and rapid change that my brain could not explain what just happened. The storm inside of me became calm in a split second. I got scared and jumped up breaking the solemnity of our prayer shouting, "AMEN. AMEN and AMEN!" Everyone knew something extraordinary had happened while we prayed and waited for an answer, but I simply said "We worship a God who hears our prayers!" because I knew that God was at work.

"His hand is not too short." My friends replied in agree-ment. Deep down, a "knowing" settled in - God has this sit-uation completely under control.

I called home to let them know that we were praying, my sister answered the phone. She was taking care of my dad for a while but then she told me she gave up. She said that my dad had become angry and rude, pushing everyone away. But she said today something had happened. He called and apologized! He confessed, despite his pride, that fear of death and pain made him weak, therefore angry and rude. He asked for her forgiveness and said he didn't want to die alone. My sister forgave him and went back to help him. Before she ended the conversation, she said, "What's interesting is that he is acting completely different now. He became calm almost as though he has inner PEACE!" She was shocked by this radical transformation in my dad's behavior. I knew it was God.

I called my dad to get his version of events. I wanted to see if he would acknowledge his new peaceful state of being. "Through prayers you are experiencing God's grace and peace!" I told him excitedly. "God is an old man, who is busy with other people. He has no time for me", he replied sadly. He felt unworthy of God's attention. Sometimes, we believe that God is like a king - powerful and inaccessible, unapproachable and unreachable. On the contrary, Jesus is available to us 24/7!

"God made the sky and the stars, and He knows them by name! You are more important to Him than anything in this world! He loves you and He sacrificed His life for you!" I passionately defended God. My dad quietly listened. It gave me confidence to press further..."Where do you want to spend your eternity Heaven or Hell? Now is the time to decide!" It's not that easy to discard God and ignore the question of Heaven or Hell when you are on your deathbed. I knew the Holy Spirit was working within him. My father asked more and more about Jesus. We talked for hours. God provided the right people, opportunities and timing to bring my dad to Jesus.

One of the many ways God brought the right people into my father's life was through my mother-in-law, of all people. She had been to Ukraine on mission trips in the past and still has connections there. A pastor there was still one of her good friends. She asked me if my dad would like to meet with him. I didn't think my dad would agree, but to my amazement, and my entire family's amazement also, he did. The pastor made time to visit my father and I was impressed that he was even able to find my dad's place, tucked away in the middle of nowhere. They spent all day in his house talking about Jesus!

Shortly after this visit, my dad passed away. No one wanted to call me with this news. No one wanted to break my heart. While taking the bus to work one day, I called home to check in and that's when they told me father was gone. On the bench, in the middle of the mall, I poured out my pain to God then called my husband. He consoled me and prayed for me, then let all our friends and family know. Slowly my tears dried up as I began receiving messages from people.

"My condolences, we are praying for you", "praying", "praying..."

I told my manager what happened, and she wanted me to take the day off. I decided to stay and work because I couldn't bear the thought of being alone. As my shift wore on though I found myself laughing at my client's jokes feeling confused and guilty. "I should be grieving... this is so sad and painful, but all I am feeling is joy and peace! God is so good!" I thought to myself.

I was grateful that I had reconciled with my father, but I was still wondering if he had accepted Christ as his Savior. I apologized to God for being such a human. I wanted reassurance, so I asked God to give me a sign to let me know that my dad was in heaven. On Sunday at the church, the lady who prayed for my dad before, asked me about him. I broke down crying, letting her know that he had passed away and that I was troubled with the question of his salvation. I was worried that even if he had accepted Christ that day with the pastor, he wouldn't have had time to build a relationship with God... that maybe a simple acceptance of God's love wasn't enough.

My wise friend comforted me by saying that God's forgiveness cannot be earned, and we certainly don't deserve it. We all fall short of the glory of God, but that Salvation is not as complicated as we think. I stopped crying. Her words lit a spark of hope in my heart. "God forgave you. Do you think He loves your father any less?" Then she pointed me to the Bible story about the thief that was crucified with Jesus who repented just hours before his death and got saved:

> One of the criminals hanging beside him scoffed, "So you're the Messiah, are you? Prove it by saving yourself—and us, too, while you're at it!". But the other criminal protested, "Don't you fear God even when you have been sentenced to die? We deserve to die for our crimes, but this man hasn't done anything wrong." Then he said, "Jesus, remember me when you come into your Kingdom." And Jesus replied, "I assure you, today you will be with me in paradise.
>
> Luke 23:39-43, NLT

This story fanned the flicker of hope I had about my dad's salvation. I thought to myself, this is an answer to my prayer! My father is forgiven! He is in heaven! The lady and I started walking downstairs. At the same time an older gentleman was coming up completely blocking our exit. He looked straight at me and said, "Hi, I don't think you know me, I'm Pastor Chris. I was talking to your mother-in-law and I just wanted to encourage you that your father is in heaven." These were his exact words. It was unreal. If you know God - this is how He works - in plain MIRACLES.

Downstairs I saw my mother-in-law, curious about what she could have told Pastor Chris to make him think my father was in heaven. I was about to tell her about the peace I had and how I really believed my father was in heaven, when she interrupted me. "I haven't had a chance to tell you yet, but I was just speaking with the pastor who visited your father. He told me that your dad was interested in how to pray and was seriously seeking answers. Your father was surprised to find out that Salvation is a gift from Jesus that can be obtained by praying a simple prayer. He prayed with the pastor that day!"

This was my final sign. That morning God told me three times that my dad was in heaven. God Almighty cares for every detail of our lives! He is a Perfect Father! I never cried for my father again. He is with God now in Heaven.

Shortly after my father died, I was speaking with my grandmother on the phone. A few minutes into the conversation I asked her if she knew my father had died. She became quiet and after a few seconds confessed that she knew but didn't know how to be the one to tell me – *she assumed I didn't know my father had died*! "I thought you didn't know! How are you so happy? I expected you to be full of sorrow, but since you are so happy I assumed you didn't know!" My poor grandmother was very confused. " I didn't lose him. I will see my father again one day in heaven. He has eternal life because he accepted God as his lord and savior!". I began explaining how simple salvation was. I told her that although I was sad my father had a terrible life without God, I was rejoicing that he accepted Him in the end. I emphasized that God always gives us the choice – he never forces us! This impacted my grandmother and she became curious.

In the past, we'd had many discussions about God. She would always argue that God had given her nothing and that everything she had she worked for herself. Her mistakes and her victories determined her destiny. I would always reply that the only reason she had breath in her lungs was because of God. The conversation would then go silent and she'd bluntly change the subject. My grandmother was my role model – I loved her and after coming to Christ I longed for her to experience the joy I had. But I also knew how stubborn she was, so I never expected her to change. After these heated conversations, I would simply remind her that being a good person wasn't going to get her into heaven and that Jesus didn't come to save *good* people. He came to save the lost and we are *all* lost – even her.

You can imagine I was surprised to find out then that my grandmother had started going to church! She even bought pictures of saints, a cross, and a candle and told me she had been praying to them. She was a little embarrassed to admit that she was seeking. Although I was excited for her to finally be open my heart was heavy. She didn't grasp the concept of God's grace; she thought praying to the saints and performing certain rituals was what she needed to do in order to earn God's favor and love. I explained that those things did nothing and that God's love could never be earned. I explained to her that it would be like me praying to her picture all the way here in Canada – no matter how earnestly I asked that picture to help me, it would never happen. The picture is not the person and was powerless to intervene. I explained that once you accept Jesus as your savior, he lives in you and you can speak with him wherever you are – direct access!

After this conversation, I was determined to visit her. Unfortunately, I was in the process of getting my Canadian citizenship and I couldn't leave the country at the time. A few weeks later I found out I was pregnant with a high risk pregnancy, so I really couldn't travel now. My grandmother got sick that year and the doctors couldn't figure out what was wrong. Even after numerous tests they couldn't explain the pain in her stomach. Her health began rapidly declining, her voice getting weaker and weaker with each phone call. I knew we didn't have much time left. I was determined that my grandmother have a chance to pray the prayer of salvation. I sat at my computer to type up a little script – something my grandmother could read and pray along with if she wanted to – but my computer froze. With desperation, I tried a few things and finally got it to print ... the printer wasn't working! I felt like something was trying to stop me from getting this prayer out. But, like my grandmother, I was stubborn and refused to give up. I called my sister begging her to write down a prayer and take it to my grandmother so she could read it. Embarrassed by my request, she refused and asked her boyfriend to do it. At this point, I didn't care *who* wrote it ... I just wanted *someone* to do it and take it my grandmother. Once he had finished writing it down, I told them to go to my grandmother's house immediately and explain what I wanted. We hung up the phone and I prayed that God would move.

The next day I called my sister to ask about my grandmother. She was silent on the other end. "Lena, I'm so sorry ... I feel awful. I'm the last person who saw her alive!". My grandmother had passed away. "But did she say the prayer!?" I asked. "Yes, yes ... although she couldn't read it herself, I read it for her and she nodded and agreed. She understood every word" my sister reassured me. In that moment, I had peace. I replied to my sister that I knew she would be waiting for me in heaven.

My husband asked me a couple days later if I was angry at God for taking away people so close to me after I had become a Christian. I pondered the question and finally answered, "No, I actually feel blessed... blessed that God used me to be the one to share Christ with them! It's a privilege beyond compare." As if to test my resolve (even though I know God doesn't test us in this way), a few months later my grandfather also passed away. After my grandmother died, he was depressed and got sick. He didn't know how to live without her and refused to eat anything or take care of himself. I tried to encourage him by explaining that she was in heaven and that he could see her one day, too. Eventually he prayed the same prayer my grandmother did a few months before he died. They are all together now and I have peace, all glory to God.

Chapter 30

Growing Family

———————✳———————

*O*ur life was pretty comfortable with just the three of us. We were growing as Christians, growing as parents, and just enjoying being a family. Things weren't perfect – they never are, of course – and I remember complaining one day to my neighbor about how hard parenting can be. He chuckled, knowing that we had only had one kid, and suggested if I thought parenting was so hard with one, I should have more kids to see how hard it really could be! Just the thought of it stressed me out. Raising our first daughter was difficult for us. She was our Guinea pig and crash course on parenting. Although we didn't know what we were doing at first, we learned along the way that discipline was crucial. Once we had that ingredient, we started to see improvements in our relationship with our daughter and with her attitude. Things had finally settled down and … I was bored! I realized I didn't have much going on, nothing to look forward to. I had to come up with something new. I declared to my husband: "We will plan a trip to Ukraine to visit my family or we should buy a house... or we could have another baby!" "BABY?" He was alarmed. "Three months of peace and you wish for another "tornado?" he asked in disbelief. I have mentioned that our firstborn was a strong-willed child. Well, I thought that after her I was ready for anything. with a little more discussion, he said "Ok, we won't plan for a baby but if God blesses us so be it." Within two months I was pregnant. The day we found out I went to pray with my little one before bed and told her we were having a baby. She was so excited and only said, "Mommy! I really want to have a baby sister! Pleeeease, can it be a little girl! Please, please, please!"

"It's not up to me, sweetheart." I looked into her beautiful face. "It's up to God. We can pray and ask, but no matter who we get we have to be grateful." I've realized the importance of talking about God. I especially want her to know that if God says YES we have to praise Him. And when God says NO we have to be grateful as well. The Lord knows what is best for us and we have to trust Him. I left her room and saw my husband standing in the hallway – he had been listing to our conversation. "Make sure this time it's a boy" he whispered as I was closing her door. I knew he would love our baby regardless of whether it was a boy or a girl, but I also knew he really wanted a son. I felt torn, my heart was aching for both my husband and my daughter to get what they wanted. I prayed that God would somehow arrange things so that neither of them were disappointed. I felt peace because I have faith that God is a miracle worker. I knew he had some-thing amazing planned.

The next day, I went to work feeling a little sick. I thought it was just pregnancy nausea, but it felt different. Then, I started to bleed. Fearing the worst, I told myself I had lost the baby. Then came the tears, then came the grief. My husband picked me up from work and took me to the hospital. I was there for hours while they did test after test. Waiting for answers was killing me and if the answer was that I had lost the baby, I didn't want to hear it. In my despair, I remembered the lesson I was trying to teach my daughter to praise God in all situations because he is in control. In the hospital I prayed and was comforted. I was able to make peace with whatever the outcome was going to be. As my tears were finally dry, the doctor came around to tell me that the only thing they could find was elevated hormone levels and that I would need to come back the next day for an ultrasound. I felt a little spark of hope that this was not the end.

At home, my husband comforted me with his love and kindness reassuring me that everything was in God's hands. I came back the next day fully surrendered to God's will and whatever the doctors were going to tell me. My ultrasound was carried out and we were ready to go over the results. The sonographer, a middle-aged lady, asked with concern if I was there alone. I told her I was, but that I was prepared to hear whatever she had to say. The woman was very gentle and carried on conversation for a little while before I interrupted and asked, "Can you just tell me if my baby is okay?" She smiled warmly and said, "Yes, your babies are fine". You know when you hear something, and you know the sound made it through your ears but it didn't quite make it into your brain? This was happening to me. "Babies?" I whispered in disbelief. Yesterday I thought I had no baby and here I am finding out I have TWO! The sonographer continued explaining and showing me the images on the screen, convincing me that, yes indeed, I was having two babies. She explained that by the difference in shape (they looked like pear and banana) it's 99% chance it's male and female. I remember my heart's cry that both my husband and my daughter would get the baby they wanted (We have no twins in any of our families). I was overwhelmed. If you were standing outside that hospital room that day, you would have thought I was crazy – there were tears, laughter, silence, more laugher, more tears, and finally praises! I felt joy, pure joy. When I called my husband to tell him, he was ecstatic but not necessarily surprised that God had come through. He told me that the night before the ultrasound, he prayed specifically for GRACE and PEACE. My mother-in-law jokes, "It's a good thing you didn't ask for grace, peace, and joy … otherwise you would have ended up with triplets!" We can laugh about this now, but it was these prayers and this reliance on God that got us through from despair to joy. Before leaving the hospital, I was warned that pregnancies involving twins are considered high risk. In many instances, one of the babies does not survive the first trimester. My joy gave way to offense. "God gave me these babies and I will deliver them both" I thought defiantly.

The moment you find out you are having twins is one of a kind and you cherish it and look back fondly at that moment for the rest of your life. The rest of the moments after that, not so much. Carrying twins is hard! I loved my first pregnancy and thought all my pregnancies would be the same. Unfortunately, this was not the case for me. I bled on and off for most of it, was diagnosed with gestational diabetes so I had to start paying special attention to what I ate and what my blood sugar levels were, and to top it all off, I got the "itch". For whatever reason, possibly hormones, my entire body felt like it was covered with poison ivy although there were no signs of a rash. I would scratch and scratch with no relief. All the itching robbed me of my sleep and decreased my appetite. I began to lose weight. The only thing that provided temporary relief was a shower and in those showers, I would cry, "Please God, as soon as these babies are ready to come out ... let them come!"

It was 11pm and my back and been hurting all day. "Great – another symptom to add to the list of this pregnancy!" Baby was asleep and my hubby was relaxing. I went to him and told him that my back pain was becoming unbearable ... that everything was becoming unbearable! He dropped what he was doing, called his mom and asked if we could take our daughter to her house so he could take me to the hospital. "The last time your back hurt like this, we had a baby!" I was only at 29 weeks, so although I wasn't sure, we went to the hospital. My husband had more urgency than me – foot on the gas pedal, flying on the night roads (thankfully, they were empty!), he jokingly told me not to have the babies in the car. We checked-in at the hospital and 2 hours later, our babies were born!

Chapter 31

Twins

"*O*ur babies were born" oh, if it were only that simple! Those four little words don't do the process justice. From day one, this was always a high-risk pregnancy. I was prepared for that and was even prepared for the babies to come early (especially when I was begging God to make it happen!). But 29 weeks was a shock... a shock to me, a shock to my husband, and even a shock to the medical staff that were working that night. Once we were checked-in and settled into a room, the chaos started. The room was flooded with people bringing charts, monitors, and other medical devices. Doctors, anesthesiologist, and nurses were all trying to find out more information about my pregnancy and myself. It dawned on me that this was an emergency! I started panicking. My heart beat so loud. I could hardly hear what they were saying. I felt so confused and scared. I remembered the trauma of childbirth – I almost died. Now, this time I was fearing for my babies' lives. Such overwhelming fear.

After some monitoring, it was decided that I should be sent to another hospital that was better suited to deliver babies in such dire circumstances. The doctor came in to check on me one last time before authorizing my transfer. I was too far in my labour; transferring me would put me at risk for delivering these babies en route to the other hospital! Frantic thoughts of death were swirling around in my head "We're going to die – all 3 of us – and my husband and my daughter will be alone". I was sick with fear and short of breath, as well as in pain from the labour. I locked eyes with my husband and asked him to pray. With my mind racing and body trembling, I began to hear his voice – strong, confident, familiar – grounding me in the hope and promises of God. I was transported to a place of tranquility. My breathing evened out, panic started to dissipate, and I became still. "Whatever happens tonight, will happen. The only way out is through and God is in control". I took a deep breath, as though God's promises were the very air I breathed. With my exhale, I opened my eyes and the storm inside me had vanished. My brain needed a few seconds to catch up with the physical change in my body. I looked around the room. What seemed chaotic and overwhelming at first, gave way to order – these were trained professionals doing their jobs. I asked the doctor what they needed from me. Question after question, I answered quickly and with clarity. They laid out a few medical options before me and I chose with precision; c-section with local anesthetics.

I was prepped and ready to deliver. My husband was looking somber. "Are you okay?" he asked. Strangely, I was okay – I really was! I marveled at this inner peace. How could I, the one who is even terrified of going to the dentist, be okay right now? And then I heard my baby's cry. "1:38am, male" and then "1:38 am, female" followed by another faint cry. Tears were pouring down my face, my babies were born!

I look back at this night and am reminded of God's faithfulness. Without him in my life, I would probably look back at this night very differently. I would remember the chaos and the fear. I would be bitter that I had to go through something so traumatic. I would focus on the worst and be caught up in the despair I felt. But no, that is not my story! Yes, there was fear, yes there were moments that felt like chaos.... but God was orchestrating everything. Instead of the fear, I remember peace. Instead of the chaos, I remember the stillness. Instead of bitterness, I cry out in gratitude – God is faithful! And if things had gone differently, if something had happened to my beautiful babies, God would still be faithful. It's the lesson I am teaching my children because it's the lesson I'm always trying to learn for myself.

Chapter 32

Hospital Life ... Again

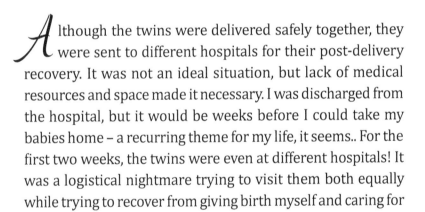

Although the twins were delivered safely together, they were sent to different hospitals for their post-delivery recovery. It was not an ideal situation, but lack of medical resources and space made it necessary. I was discharged from the hospital, but it would be weeks before I could take my babies home – a recurring theme for my life, it seems.. For the first two weeks, the twins were even at different hospitals! It was a logistical nightmare trying to visit them both equally while trying to recover from giving birth myself and caring for my oldest one on top of it all.

I was in a lot of pain and exhausted for most of our visits, but my need to be there for my babies compelled me. When my husband had to return to work, I braved the drive all by myself (even the highway! I had only gotten my full license a month before the babies were born). I couldn't take painkillers because those made me drowsy, but my reward was holding my children. He didn't approve, but I couldn't be stopped. My babies needed to know they were loved, cared for, and *wanted*.

When I saw my daughter for the first time she looked just like her sister, dark hair, dark skin, and dark eyes. Seeing this little bundle through the incubator glass and watching how the nurses handled her needs was fascinating. Babies really aren't as fragile as you think! When I saw my son for the first time I was shocked – were they sure this little blonde bundle was mine? He had white skin, blonde hair and blue eyes! My favourite times were when I was allowed to hold my babies up against my skin. The nurses encouraged this type of contact as it encourages the baby to strive more; they develop faster and healthier. What a beautiful thought! Such a simple gesture, but one with profound meaning and worth. They were so tiny that sometimes I would have both of them on my chest at the same time! I felt their calm breathing and the warmth of their tiny bodies. I could hear their faint hearts beating together rhythmically. With every movement of their body, I would hold my breath. God made mothers heart so big! I'm amazed that I can love them both the same, but also so uniquely.

It took me five weeks to recover from surgery. I wasn't resting properly and kept driving to be with my babies. People were asking me how I could bear to be apart from my newborns. But, as I've told you, I had so much peace. God was in control then and he is in control now! He used that hospital staff to bless me and in return I prayed that God would bless them triple and quadruple amounts for all the love and care they are providing for those babies and their families.

Although bringing those babies home after 6 weeks felt like the end of a chapter, it was really just the beginning of the next. Becoming parents to three kids was not – and is not – easy! Everything we thought we knew about ourselves and how to raise a family was about to change. But, one thing I know. Having three kids with God is easier than having one without!

Chapter 33

Growing Passions

——————✳——————

When I was a kid my grandma would tell us grand-kids to go and pick flowers or climb a tree for its blossoms. She paid us with candy to make it worth our while and along the way she would explain the healing proper-ties of the particular plants we were collecting, sparking my lifelong interest in naturopathy. On one occasion, my grandpa -drunk at the time – grabbed my face, and with tears streaming down his face, said I looked just like his mother whenever he saw me out picking flowers. "She was a village healer but people called her a witch. They were scared of her abilities." He said sadly. People back home were bound by such superstitions and after this conver-sation I believed that I had supernatural abilities to heal people! Once my friend had a tooth ache and with "abraca-dabra" moves and a loud command for her pain to go away I healed her! I was so impressed that it worked. I believed I was special. From then on, I wanted to stand out.

You have to understand that when I was growing up, people in my country were very poor. To provide for our family (on top of working hours) we had to plant, grow, harvest, and preserve our own food. We had small live stock as well. Most of our healthcare needs we took care of at home with natural remedies. Grandma had a solution and protocol for every situation that she passed down to each generation. When I came to Canada, I embraced the English language, culture and even western medicine, but I couldn't help pointing out plants and their medical abilities to all my friends. It was in my blood. "If you cut yourself, this plant can be used as a bandage. It usually grows by the path in the forest and has the ability to stop the bleeding and disinfect the wound as well." I would announce proudly. "Or here is the tree called Lipa. Flowers from it make a great remedy for cold and cough in the winter." And I would show my friends how to collect it. "Right here are wild raspberries..." and I'd eat some right from the bush. Each time my friends would tell me I was crazy. Sometimes they'd say that my country was underdeveloped and that we were way behind on medical advancements. I would get embarrassed, so I tried to fit in and turned away from my grandma's wisdom. I mean, some of her recipes did sound crazy.... "It's ok grandma, we have Tylenol for that ..." I began brushing off her advice.

When I first came to Canada, I was smitten by the amount of food in the supermarket all year, all beautifully displayed in order to attract more customers. The displays were gorgeous, but after eating the fruit from them for a while, I found myself disappointed. None of the fruits or vegetables tasted quite right. They were lacking the specific flavor and aroma of home.

Fruits and vegetables aside, I had an easy life here compared to back home. No more hard work, sweat, pain and dirt. Then another glorious discovery! Special cleaners, new chemicals, special dusters, mopping, laundry detergent and dryer sheets that smelled very powerful and cleaned without any hassle. I told my husband, "Who needs to waste their time, breaking their backs cleaning? You spray chemicals and it's done!". Like many others I was "sold" an easy lifestyle and I loved it. No more washing clothes and hanging them outside to dry for hours. No more mopping and touching dirty rags with my hands. No more vinegar and soap for cleaning the glass. Now it's nice, fast and easy. It worked for a while, but I started to notice that I would have headache right after cleaning. And the smell of chemicals stayed for a long time. I could smell them even when I wasn't using anything (from the closed closet). When my daughter was two she went to day care and I was back at work full time. For the first three months my firstborn brought home every possible virus. She got ear infections and went through three rounds of antibiotics. I had to give her Tylenol/ Advil every three hours for days without the fever going away completely. I went to the doctors and sat for countless hours in the emergency room. My husband and I suffered from our own health problems, too. The worst was our honeymoon when he had a horrible sinus infection. He took a turn for the worse on our flight down, so we saw a doctor as soon as we landed. His advice: "No sun, no diving, and no alcohol". He was disappointed, but I was glad he wasn't in the hospital or worse, the cemetery! While my husband suffered from sinus infections, I often got bronchitis. So often, I was misdiagnosed with asthma. Antibiotic after antibiotic, nothing helped. I later realized that I was a little naïve to trust the doctors so completely with my health! Turns out, the doctor who prescribed rounds of antibiotics in a row did lose his license. I felt like a fool. Something needed to change.

My sister-in-law was ahead of me experimenting with different health products investing money and trying to improve her lifestyle naturally. After many "hit and miss" products she discovered and introduced me to essential oils. "What is your number one health concern?" she asked me excitedly as she opened her wooden treasure box full of oils. I was already hooked "Respiratory issues". I said. She pulled out a respiratory blend and opened the bottle. The scent was pleasant and powerful and it made me wary. It reminded me of the synthetic dryer sheets that made me sick. She put one drop into my hand and told me to breath it in, so I did. To my amazement it didn't make me sick! The opposite happened, my lungs felt great. I took another deep breath inhaling this wonderful aroma. This is what I was looking for, a natural, safe, and effective solution. I researched further how I could improve my family's well-being. Slowly I replaced all the chemicals in my home. I fell in love with the company, products, and community. My twins were born and at seven month I was oiling them up like there was no tomorrow. Essential oils provided me with natural solutions and empowered me as a mom. I know I am healing my family and people around me. When my three kids went to full time grade 4 and JK in public school, I knew their immune system needed an extra boost. I used a variety of oils to help support their immune system. The result? No stomach flu (some families from our classes went through it twice, and I heard numerous health complaints from other moms) no flu, no colds, no antibiotics, no sleepless nights! With five people in the house our sick days are now few, even my husband's notorious sinus infections are less often now. The oils help the body's natural ability to heal itself. I was invigorated by this discovery of a new passion. Although it was new to me, in many ways it felt like I was returning to my roots and the ancient knowledge that was passed down to me. I had always loved making people feel beautiful as a hairstylist, but now I discovered that I could also help people live a more healthy life, too!

Chapter 34

Return to Ukraine

$\int$ t had been 10 years – 10 whole years since I had been home. There was so much in my life that was different, I found myself aching to return and reconnect with my family in person. I wanted them to see the new person that I was and the family I had created. I spoke with my husband and we decided it was a good time to visit my family back in Ukraine. We always knew traveling with three kids wasn't going to be easy and we were right. From beginning to end, my journey 'home' was full of ups and downs, curves, and unexpected twists. Looking back, I can say everything worked out and the trip was worth it but in the middle of it, I couldn't help but think we had made a horrible decision.

First, the trip started with two very sick twins. One sick baby on a plane is enough to derail even the most prepared parent, but two?! Then, I discovered that I hadn't packed enough formula – a simple miscalculation that led to some very cranky babies as I tried to supplement the formula with food they weren't quite used to. Add to the mix a very social

6-year-old and husband who can't speak the language and you have a recipe for disaster. Once we had arrived – shockingly in one piece – we found out that our living arrangements had fallen through. The apartment we had planned on staying in was no longer available. Thankfully, we were able to find a one-bedroom bachelor that would do the trick, even if it was a tight squeeze. It was a four-story walk-up on the other side of town of my family – far from ideal, but like I said, it did the trick and did have a pretty view of the river – it's one redeeming quality.

I'm not sure what I expected my trip home to be like. All I knew was that I wanted my family to see the difference in my life and come to know Christ, the reason for my difference! Before leaving, I built up so much hope and expectation around them accepting Christ. I was so eager to share my faith and just thought that if I did, they would accept Jesus, too. Thankfully, I shared these desires with people I trust. Those people cautioned me not to pressure my family or force a change they weren't ready for. My mother-in-law told me, "just go there and live out your faith. They knew you before and will see the difference. Look for opportunities and pray about it".

It was nice to be with my family, but I hadn't realized the comforts of Canada that I had gotten used to. Raising three kids in Canada is tiring, but at least we have the convenience of a car, a vacuum, dishwasher, laundry machine, dryer – so many labour-saving devices! Here, it took 2 days for our clothes to dry because it was so humid. I wasn't used to that anymore. My family laughed at me – they didn't know what a life of convenience felt like. They reminded me that I was lucky to even have hot water – most of the city was still without.

It was a few days in before I realized that I was experiencing culture shock. I looked around at the city before me and it was not the city of my memory. Buildings were crumbling, infrastructure was wanting, and everything seemed old. I was so disappointed! I was also starting to get self-conscious about my English-speaking husband – what if people knew he didn't speak Russian and tried to take advantage of him? I know what people, especially desperate people, are capable of. And finally – what if someone from my past found out I was home? I was dreading that at any moment someone from my past would recognize me and call me a fraud for the life I was now living. Fear started creeping in, followed by regret. "What was I thinking coming back here?!" I asked myself a dozen times every day. I'm embarrassed to say that I forgot my mission in even going. All I wanted was my family to see a different me. So far, they were getting an exhausted version of myself who was struggling to find meaning in even being there.

All the nice family get togethers I had envisioned where I could share my testimony often devolved into conflict halting any chance for discussion of faith. There was drunkenness, verbal abuse, and even physical abuse – all things that, growing up, were very familiar to me. Back then it was normal, but now I saw it as brokenness … brokenness I wanted nothing to do with. It's funny how your perspective on things can change – what was once as familiar to you as an old pair of sneakers, worn in from years of use, now feel like hard wooden clogs. You begin to wonder how you even walked around in those shoes for so long and with this new perspective, you start to see the toll those wooden shoes had on you. Blisters in the shape of broken relationships… calluses of anger, fear and resentment… sores of loneliness that developed into a lack of self-worth. Is it any wonder I limped through life? "On your feet wear the Good News of peace to help you stand strong" Ephesians 10:15. The armor of God has always been a powerful image for me, and it seems fitting here again. Jesus took my wooden clogs and fitted me with shoes so I could run freely!

For the last week of our time, we decided to go to the Black Sea with my family as a vacation for all of us. We stayed in small cabins and were served delicious food. Our time there was more peaceful, a nice break from our four-story walk-up in the rundown city. The kids loved being in the water, we were getting nice tans, and we finally felt like we were relaxing ... until my hubby got food poisoning. Him getting sick was the last straw for me – I broke down. I grumbled to God, "It was crazy to come here! We spent all this money and time to be sick, uncomfortable, and stressed! I have to wash clothes by hand, bathe my kids in a bucket, take cold showers and have no rest at all! What the heck am I am doing here?" I then realized it was the first time I had actually taken time to reach out to God since going home. Not once in all of my discomfort and despair did I actually turn to him, instead I dwelled on the circumstances before me and threw myself a pity party. Well, once I invited God to my pity party he showed up and shut it down. He reminded me that I was only visiting, but that these people live here. He reminded me that I was to be a witness for Him – to show his love, his grace, his peace, his wholeness. He reminded me that the things I were crying over – inconsequential things like comforts and conveniences – were nothing compared to the eternal value of knowing him. He showed me that by looking at myself, I had missed out on all the blessings he had scattered throughout our trip that

I completely overlooked. We had the means to travel, all five of us, to a foreign country without going into debt. I was able to share a piece of my history with my husband that increased our intimacy. I was reconciled to my family and they cared and fed for us as well as they knew how. It was there that our twins took their first bites of solid food and even took their first steps. We met cousins and family members I had only seen in pictures. Lastly, my family was asking about Jesus! This trip was a success.

As my pity party came to an end while I reflected on all the positives things that happened in our trip, the sky cracked open and rain started to pour. It lasted for only a few minutes, and then stopped as suddenly as it had started. A huge double rainbow appeared in the sky. I started to cry. I took it as a sign that I am never alone. God loves me! He never leaves me, never forsakes me, and never gives up on me. He showed me the way when I was lost and will continue to show me the way when I lose the path again. After my time of solitude, I went back to family and found my oldest one and her cousin jumping in the puddles. All the kids were laughing with joy, fascinated at the beautiful rainbow in the sky. In that moment, I snapped a photo of the kids on either end of the rainbow pretending to hold it. I cherish this photo as a reminder of the relationships I'm continuing to build with my family.

Chapter 35

Olga

*A*fter my trip to Ukraine, I kept thinking about how I could continue to talk to my family about God. I so wanted for my family to fall in love with God, like I had. One day, I came across a beautiful Bible. It was very large print, full of pictures, and was written in Russian. I thought that this would make a perfect gift for my family. I bought it for them and even underlined verses that stood out to me. This book had changed my life – still changes my life every time I read it! It was such a beautiful experience reading the Bible in my native language. Although I was already very familiar with it English, reading it in Russian brought it alive to me in new ways and I wanted my family to share this experience.

I got ready to send them this Russian Bible that I had gotten so fond of, but the thought occurred to me ... what if they don't care for it? What if they destroy it?! I imagined my sister's kids ripping the pages out, while the adults used the discarded pages as rolling paper for their cigarettes. I shuddered at the thought. No, this was too precious a thing for them to destroy; it must be protected. It was my job to defend and protect His Word, I thought to myself. But I felt a little nudge in my spirit. "God doesn't need you to defend or protect Him. He just wants you to share Him". Again, as I had done in Ukraine, I made things all about me and my comfort. So, although I really did not want to, I ended up mailing my family this precious Bible.

When I mailed it to them, I explained what this book did for me and how important it is. How there is so much wisdom in the pages and how it's God's guide for our lives. I asked them to treat it with respect and read it if they were interested. They've had it for a while, and the last we spoke, they still haven't read it. "It's too big – a little intimidating" they say. But I trust that this is a small seed that God will grow into something, like the picture Bible my bodyguard gave me in Israel.

They may not read the Bible I sent them, but they do read my letters. Writing letters to them is something I have always done. My grandma especially loved it, as Skype and e-mail were too advanced for her to get used to. She always liked having something tangible, something she could carry around and re-read if she wanted to. Unfortunately, my grandma has passed but it was a little after her death that I realized the potential for my letters home. If my family won't read the Bible because it's too intimidating, I'll put the Bible in my letters which they read all the time! So, there I was writing full pages of the Bible to my family with the hopes that somehow the life in those words would be contagious.

After sending a few letters, I finally asked my family what they had thought. They said they liked the ones they got, but that there were only a few that actually made it to them. My family told me that since they have one big community mailbox, sometimes other people take their mail, open it, and never return it. I guess the good news was that *someone* was reading the Bible in my letters, but the bad news was that it wasn't my family!

I was little disappointed, but I didn't let this stop me. I had another idea. I knew that my cousin, Olga, lived in a house that had a secure mailbox. If I could send letters to her, she could give them directly to my closer family members. Not that Olga and I weren't close, in fact, we had always been very close as children. She was my favourite and closest of cousins – I even taught her how to swim! But, time and distance caused us to grow apart and when I was in Ukraine with my family, I didn't get to really connect with her in the way I had hoped. I was worried that this was a relationship that might never get repaired.

With all these anxious thoughts, I had no choice but to call her. My goal was to get my family reading the Bible through my letters and this was the best chance I had of accomplishing that goal. Things with Olga were so strained that I didn't even think she'd talk to me on the phone, let alone be my own personal mailman! Regardless of my fears, I strongly felt I just *had* to call her. "Just be obedient", I heard a voice tell me.

I nervously dialed her number, held my breath as the phone rang and rang with no answer. When I finally thought she wouldn't answer, I heaved a sigh of relief, "phew – dodged that bullet!" but then, the line connected. I heard a voice on the other line, "Hello? Who is this?". I tensed up and for a second and remained silent. "Hello? Who is this?" she repeated. I slowly said who was calling, afraid she wouldn't stay on the line, but to my surprise, she said she was glad to hear from me! Warm memories and love flooded my heart for this woman. I know we had lost touch, but she was good to me when I was a troubled teenager. I longed to be reconciled with her.

We chatted for a while and I asked if she could pass out the letters to my family. She agreed, but was curious about what was in the letters. "What was so important that my family just had to read it?" she asked. I told her that I put some Bible verses in the letters and it's my hope that my family would read them and learn about Jesus. She said that she would like one of these letters, too. My heart start pounding, "Would you like to know more about Jesus?" I asked carefully but with excitement in my voice.

For two hours, I told her all about God and the change in me. I told her about God's love, His mercy, Jesus' sacrifice for our sin, and Salvation. I told her how much I treasured my relationship with Christ, that He loved me first and died for me even when I didn't know or love Him back. She kept saying that she never knew this, that she had never heard it explained like that. I then told her that receiving Christ into your life was as simple as a little prayer. I asked if she wanted to pray with me and to my amazement, she said yes! . "Whosoever calls on the name of the Lord shall be saved."(Romans 10:13) I started praying. What I thought was going to be a very awkward phone call turned out to be one of the most beautiful moments of my life; I witnessed a person give their life to Christ! We hung up the phone and I did a little happy dance, praising God for the miracles he does.

A few short weeks later, I got a phone call. Olga had passed away suddenly from a blood clot in her brain. This young woman, only 28 years old, was gone. My family knew how important Olga had been to me and knew that we had reconnected, so they didn't know how to break the news to me. When they called to tell me, I was heartbroken, but I remembered our conversation on the phone and how we had prayed together. I know I will see Olga again. We can't prevent death or avoid it. We don't know how much time we really have. Life is precious and unpredictable, but we do have control of our decisions. We can decide to accept Christ or reject him for eternity. I thank God that Olga choose Jesus.

Chapter 36

New Beginnings

*A*fter we settled back in from Ukraine, my husband and I decided it was time to buy a house. We were still living in a 2-bedroom apartment with three kids. The living arrangements were getting tight as our kids were getting older and we wanted space for our children to grow up. At the same time, his company moved to a new warehouse in another city and it was taking him forever to get home in the evenings, so we decided that wherever we were going to move it had to be closer to his work.

Excited at the thought of being home owners, we found a real estate agent and began checking listings. I thought this whole process was going to be so wonderful and that it would bring my husband and I closer together as we planned for our future. I was wrong – it sucked! We were fighting, arguing and couldn't agree on anything except the budget. We found nothing, even after searching for three months and seeing fifty houses. We were getting so frustrated, so I started praying for God to help us. I was waiting for a miracle and my husband was getting impatient. I had my list of things we needed and was often disappointed when many of the houses we looked at didn't meet the criteria. After a while, my hubby and the realtor told me to adjust my expectations because it was unlikely that we would ever find anything that was 'perfect'. This would make me upset, because I always felt like something special was right around the corner. You see, I didn't just want a house. I wanted a *home*.

We were down to our last three houses before we were going to give up. One of them was really nice with a finished basement. I even began envisioning where I could put a salon. But just as I was starting to feel like this could be it, my husband reminded me it was over our budget. The realtor didn't correct him – it really was over our budget. We saw another house, a bigger one this time. I loved it, but it was even more over our budget and had a long list of things that needed fixing. Thinking we'd be able to negotiate the price a little because of the issues, we put it an offer. It was refused and we starting to get hopeless. On the way home my husband and I began squabbling about all our wasted time. We started to feel like we were never going to find a house.

When we got home, the squabbling turned into a full-blown argument about how we weren't on the same page. I felt like he was saying it was my fault because my expectations were too high. I was hurt and felt like he didn't understand. Just when I thought we were going to make up, he sarcastically offered to help me 'adjust my expectations'. Waves of new anger washed over my body – I hadn't felt such anger in a long time, it caught me off guard. I was trembling with rage and in that moment, I really wanted to hurt him. If it were a few years ago, I might have done just that. Given my childhood, I could easily imagine escalating this argument to a physical fight... but Jesus. I reminded myself I was a new creation and didn't have to lash out. I decided to walk away and pray. I needed to collect myself and pray for God's peace and his wisdom for how to move forward. After praying, I was calm enough to go to sleep thinking we'd deal with this in the morning.

Every morning, I prepare my husband's breakfast and pack him a lunch. When I woke up the morning after our big fight, I thought to myself there was no way I would do that for him today – he could make his own breakfast and lunch and adjust *his* expectations about *that*! But again... Jesus. The holy spirit challenged me to be a loving wife, despite my hurt. Fine, I'd make him lunch ... but it would be a sloppy one, I bargained. *No, make him a good lunch.* I sighed and with that began preparing him a good lunch like I do every day. He was surprised when I handed him his lunch like everything was normal. "Oh, I didn't do this for *you* - I'm trying to be obedient over here!" I reassured him, wanting to emphasize I still wasn't happy with our fight. A few hours later, he texted me an apology and we reconciled. That's the amazing thing about Jesus. Here I was thinking I was just making my husband a lunch, but I was really doing the groundwork of repairing our relationship by the prompting of the holy spirit. God uses everything in our lives to grow us if we only listen. "And we know that in all things God works for the good of those who love him, who have been called according to his purpose." Romans 8:28 NIV

That same day, after my husband and I had put the kids to bed, we were hanging out on the couch together scrolling through house listings online. I came across a house that made me stop, it was a house #50 we saw recently. As I looked more closely at the listing, I saw that it met all our criteria. I showed it to my hubby and asked him why we never considered this house. He assumed it was because it was out of our budget, but the it turns out this house was actually under our budget. He jumped up and called our agent and told her to put an offer on the house. The next day he went to do the inspection, and everything came up fine. Before I knew it, the house was ours ... bought from the comfort of our own home! I knew that God would provide for us exactly what we needed. It can be hard to trust Him in times of waiting and it can be tempting to take things into our own hands, but I'm glad we waited. Once the home-owners found out we were a young family buying our first house, they even lowered the price for us! We couldn't have arranged that ourselves – it was all God's provision. When we met to sign everything, the family told us all about the neighborhood – lots of parks, good schools, kind neigh-bours. This house turned out to be even more than we had imagined. I shouldn't be surprised. That's what God does. He knows your heart and knows your dreams, then blows you away with what he has planned for you.

Buying our first house was a significant moment in my life. I looked back at how far I had come and couldn't believe my life. I came from nothing and now had a beautiful family and a nice, safe home for all of us to build memories in. I'm especially thankful for our new home because it led us to our new church family. I loved our old church – it was where I met Jesus and it will forever hold a special place in my heart – so I was worried about where would find a church when we moved. Finding our new church wasn't easy. My husband and I drafted a list of places to check out, but we got so busy with settling in that a month had passed and we hadn't visited a single church. My mother-in-law, always so encouraging, told us not to give up. That day an old family friend got in touch and invited us to their church. I didn't really have the energy and the church wasn't on our list, but it was only 10 minutes away, so I said yes to be polite. When we got there, we were welcomed with open arms. Our kids were excited to attend the kid's program and registering them was very efficient. It can be hard visiting new churches! You don't know how things work or where things are, so you don't ask question and end up in the middle of the sanctuary barely able to listen to the pastor because you're trying to keep your kids quiet! Already, I felt like this was our church.

After service, the family friend came to talk to us and introduce us to some people so we could be connected. Her mom was my husband's babysitter when he was a kid! It's funny how we return to our roots sometimes. The lady who used to babysit him also greeted us and introduced us to some other people as well saying, "I changed this boy's diapers!" as she patted my 6-foot tall husband on the back. My husband, with his arms full of his own kids, laughed, saying that now he was changing diapers! Right from the start we fit in and knew this would be our new church family. I signed the kids up for some programs, got involved in some Bible studies, and even signed myself up for the woman's retreat. In fact, it was at one of these retreats that I felt the stirrings to write this book.

Chapter 37

This Book

"*G*o, what's your book about and how long have you wanted to write this book?" asked the publisher. I sighed, "I don't want to write this book!" ... probably not the answer the publisher was expecting! I continued, "Look, I prefer to keep my past to myself but ... it looks like God wants me to write this book and I want to be obedient. It's a book about God's miracles in my life – his faithfulness, unending love, and amazing grace...". As I continued talking about my vision for this book, excitement was welling up inside me and I couldn't stop talking. The publisher interrupted me, "Great – I can't wait to read it! These are the best kind of stories". That was the moment my book became real. For a while the idea of writing a book had bounced around in my head. I knew God was asking me to share my story. I didn't want to share my story, but I wanted to be obedient to God. But, now I had accountability. My book was no longer just an idea I could talk about, but something that I had to start writing.

It all began at a women's retreat where I learned the power of personal stories. The speaker was a woman from Launch, an organization that helps Christian young adults launch their ideas for sharing the Gospel. She's an amazing speaker and great at encouraging people to share their stories of God's faithfulness. I have plenty of those, so it was a great weekend of remembering how God has always been there for me. At one point in the weekend, the speaker put us into smaller groups and asked us to share times when God had intervened in our lives somehow. I spoke about the time God helped me pass by driver's license exam the month before my twins were born, which was just when I was a baby Christian learning to trust God and follow him. After we shared in the smaller groups, we were given a chance to share with the whole group. When the microphone was coming near me, I felt a prompting that I should share this story. I panicked. Public speaking is not my forte. I froze, thinking my story was embarrassing and silly. I told myself that people wouldn't understand me because of my accent. But I couldn't deny the prompting. I stood up and shared my story about passing my driver's test. As my story went on, I realized that no one even noticed that my voice was shaking and that my body was trembling like a leaf, all they heard was an awesome story of God's faithfulness. When I was finished, people thanked me for sharing and complimented my speaking abilities. Me? Speaking abilities? All glory to God. Trust is a hard thing for me, but slowly I'm learning to lean on God and trust his leading. His plans are always for our good. So, I was scared when it felt like God was asking me to share *more*. I mean, I had only just gotten comfortable sharing these little stories ... and now I had to share everything?

"You are just like me - a storyteller! You should travel and tell people your testimony." Our speaker said to me when I pulled her aside and spent a few minutes with her. "Oh no, I'm a mom with three kids – traveling is off-limits for me!" I gave as an excuse, but really, I was just afraid. "Well, then maybe you should write a book!". Laughing her off, I nervously replied that maybe I would and the seed was planted.

The next morning at breakfast I was sitting with a friend who is a published author. We were just having small talk while we ate, but my brain was shouting at me "ASK HER ABOUT THE BOOK! ASK ABOUT THE BOOK!". This pressure to ask about the book was hard to ignore, so I just blurted out "I'm thinking of a writing a book…". Immediately I felt stupid. I was afraid my friend, a real author, would ridicule me. But instead of ridicule, she oozed with encouragement, "Oh, I think you should!" and she explained the process of writing and getting published to me. The seed was being watered.

When my friend left, I asked God why he wanted me to write this book. I wasn't volunteering to do this, so I really wanted to know why now? Why share my story? My life was going so well. People knew me as an accomplished hairstylist and loving mother to three kids. I went to church and participated in Bible studies. They didn't need to know anything about my past. I could just continue sharing stories about how God is good to me *now*. He answered in a vision. I saw faces of all different types of people reacting to my story. Some were silent, some were shocked – jaws to the floor-, some were laughing, some were crying, but all of them were touched by the story of God's faithfulness. In that moment I knew that God was going to use my story to show people they are not alone and that if only one person needed to hear that, it was worth it. After this weekend, I went home and started writing what would become this book.

Chapter 38

Alpha

*O*nce we got settled into our new church, I began looking for ways to volunteer my time and use my abilities to serve others. I continued volunteering at my old church once a month cutting hair for families in the community with low income, but I felt a burning desire to do more in my own community. As opportunities came up, I considered them, but nothing felt right. I continued praying about it until one day they announced our church would be running the Alpha program. I thought back to how this course changed my life by teaching me about God in a safe, non-judgmental environment. Something in my heart was moving, but I still had my doubts. I had already done the Alpha course a few times before, so I felt silly signing up to volunteer to be a part of it again. As I wrestled with my doubts, I reminded myself that doubt, fear, and confusion never come from God, so I decided to sign up. I love to meet new people, share stories, and of course, eat good food, so I knew I'd have a good time and I was trusting God to use me.

When you sign up for the course, you are put into groups where you are encouraged to discuss and question the topics. There were a few people at my table, but a couple I had never seen before caught my attention. They were born and raised Catholics. This beautiful young lady was questioning and challenging everything in the video. As she questioned, I could feel the anger and frustration was rooted deeply in her soul. Then she told us her story full of hurt, pain, death, and unanswered prayers. No wonder she had no faith. Listening to my testimonies about God's work and His presence in my life made her uneasy. There was one time where she got up and walked away crying after something I had shared. I felt terrible, thinking it was my fault that I had hurt this woman, but God gently reminded me, "It's not you she is wrestling. It's Me." I knew there was spiritual warfare. Her friend, who brought her to Alpha lovingly and patiently poured Jesus into her heart for the last 8 years. I knew this was the right place and the right time for her to question God and try reaching out to Him. I knew it would take a long time and tons of love to heal this woman's broken heart, but I also knew it was possible – I'm living proof of that!

After one of the sessions, the couple finally decided to give their lives to Christ. We prayed with them and blessed them with prayers. I was so excited that they took this step! After we prayed, the woman shared with me, "You know, sometimes when you would share your stories I wanted to punch you in the face!" The table got quiet and a little awkward. I replied, "I know" as I looked right into her eyes "but I didn't take it personally. You weren't upset with me, you were upset with God". We embraced, with tears running down our faces, as I told her how honored I felt to be a part of this woman's life and witness her transformation. She encouraged me to keep sharing about God's faithfulness in my life and then she shared this with me:

I came home after the last session so angry at God that He had worked in someone else's life but never did anything for me even when I begged Him to. I said to God: "Show me that You are real! Prove it that you hear me and that You care for me! Do something outrageous that seeing it all I could say it's God!" Later that week my parents called and said they won the lottery – one million dollars – and that they were giving us a new house and putting a trust fund aside for our children! For so long, all I had prayed for a home and stability for my children. This is outrageous, but what's even crazier, this isn't the first time my parents won the lottery! They also won it in 1983... who wins the lottery twice?! I knew it was God. I asked him to move mountains and he did "Ask and it will be given to you; seek and you will find; knock and the door will be opened to you." Matthew 7:7 NIV

I was amazed with this story. Yes, God gave her material blessings but that wasn't what won her over. It was the fact that God was listening and knew her heart. After that I started to see them regularly at church. They radiate joy, peace, and love. I shared this story because I want to highlight how God works! He takes something broken then restores it, breaths new life, love and hope into it again, and redeems everything! No matter what our story is. His love is everlasting. "Neither height nor depth, nor anything in creation, will be able to separate us from the love of God that is in Christ Jesus our Lord". Romans 8:39 NIV

Chapter 39

Epilogue

I called my book "Miraculous".
Definition: 1. Performed by or involving a supernatural power or agency. 2. Of the nature of a miracle; marvelous.

This is the only word I can think of to describe my life and how God saved me and redeemed my story. Without this book my past would have remained 'unfinished business', an area of my mind I wouldn't willingly explore and share. I always had hope that in writing this, I would find a way to make peace with my past. Having finished this book, not only have I made peace but I've received so much healing. The areas of my life I thought were too dark to talk about have had the light turned on.

(The light shines in the darkness, and the darkness has not overcome it. John 1:5 NIV)

When that light, Jesus, shines I realize that instead of empty and broken, I am whole; instead of lonely, I am cherished, instead of hopeless, I have hope. Jesus has exchanged my shame for joy, taken my fears and insecurities and given me peace. I was once an angry, selfish woman, I am now peaceful and seek to serve others by sharing the love that I have found. The miracle is this transformation! If you had told me back when I was still living in Ukraine that one day I'd end up in Canada with a loving husband, 3 healthy kids, and a hairstyling business I would have laughed in your face. If you told me when I was working as a prostitute in Israel that one day I'd be advocating for victims of human trafficking through organizations like Fight 4 Freedom and Operation Underground Railroad I would have called you crazy. If you had told me when I first came to Canada and was struggling to learn English, that I'd one day write a book and speak to large groups of people about my life, I probably would have taken you to the psychologist myself! You see, only God can redeem our broken past and make beauty from ashes.

I don't deserve the life I now have – the peace, joy, loving husband, healthy kids, and beautiful home. It's ALL because of God. Not because of what I have done but because of Who He is. My purpose is to show you Jesus through eyes of a wicked sinner who has been saved, redeemed and justified. I understand that without the knowledge of my past you will never grasp the weight and vastness of sin that has been forgiven me. I am here to tell you: God does not make exceptions! Salvation is a gift for everyone! If He did this for me, He will do it for you! He loved me in my darkest hour. He sacrificed His Life for me... I don't deserve it and I couldn't earn it. I was wicked and I loved it. For all that I've done in my life, I should be punished ... *but God*...the two words at the heart of the Gospel!

"It wasn't so long ago that you were mired in that old stagnant life of sin. You let the world, which doesn't know the first thing about living, tell you how to live. You filled your lungs with polluted unbelief, and exhaled disobedience. We all did, all of us doing what we felt like doing, when we felt like doing it, all of us in the same boat. It's a wonder God didn't loose His temper and does away with the whole a lot of us. Instead, immense in mercy and with an incredible love, He embraced us. He took our sin-dead lives and made us alive in Christ. He did all this on His own, with no help from us! Then He picked us up and set us down in highest heaven in company with Jesus, our Messiah. Now God has us where He wants us, with all the time in this world and the next to shower grace and kindness upon us in Christ Jesus. Saving is all His idea, and all His work. All we do is trust Him enough to let Him do it. It's God's gift from start to finish! We don't play the major role. If we did, we'd probably go around bragging that we'd done the whole thing! No, we neither make nor save ourselves. God does both the making and saving. He creates each of us by Christ Jesus to join Him in the work He does, the good work He has gotten ready for us to do, work we had better be doing."

The Message. Ephesians 2:4-10.

CPSIA information can be obtained
at www.ICGtesting.com
Printed in the USA
FFHW021825090919
54842885-60535FF